Scrapbooking Your Family History

Scrapbooking Your Family History

Laura Best

Sterling Publishing Co., Inc. New York

A Sterling/Chapelle Book

Chapelle, Ltd.:
 Jo Packham
 Sara Toliver
 Cindy Stoeckl

Editor: Laura Best
Copy Editor: Marilyn Goff
Book Design: Dan Emerson,
 Pinnacle Marketing

If you have any questions or comments,
please contact:
 Chapelle, Ltd., Inc.
 P.O. Box 9252
 Ogden, UT 84409
 (801) 621-2777
 (801) 621-2788 Fax
 e-mail:
 chapelle@chapelleltd.com
 Web site: chapelleltd.com

Library of Congress Cataloging-in-
Publication Data Available

10 9 8 7 6 5 4 3 2 1
Published by
Sterling Publishing Co., Inc.
387 Park Avenue South, New York, NY 10016
©2005 by Laura Best
Distributed in Canada by Sterling Publishing
c/o Canadian Manda Group, 165 Dufferin Street
Toronto, Ontario, Canada M6K 3H6
Distributed in Great Britain by Chrysalis Books Group PLC
The Chrysalis Building, Bramley Road, London W10 6SP, England
Distributed in Australia by Capricorn Link (Australia) Pty. Ltd.
P.O. Box 704, Windsor, NSW 2756, Australia
Printed and Bound in China
All Rights Reserved

ISBN 1-4027-1658-3

Preface

Piecing Families Together

Family of Henry Edward, 1875–1973 & Lillie Adams Hennessey, 1884–1971

Inspired by the traditions and stories of my ancestors, I have developed this instructional volume of genealogical scrapbooking to encourage others to search out their grandparents and the stories of their heritage. The combination of scrapbooking and genealogy creates a beautiful heirloom while preserving historical information for future generations.

The process of researching, and studying your ancestors' lives, followed by designing a scrapbook page about their accomplishments, heartaches, and joys, solidifies in your mind their being, temperament, goals, and life experiences. This process links you emotionally and spiritually with your ancestors while preserving the legacy of your family.

Throughout the instructions in this book, "family" applies to all generations. As you begin documenting your family, start with yourself and work backward in time to your parents' and your grandparents' lives. Work with the different themes presented in this book, asking the same questions of each generation. For example, "What was Christmas morning like for you?" This is a general question to ask of you,

your parents, their parents, and so forth. Search out the trials, joys, personalities, events, and emotions of each generation in each situation.

My hope is that something will stir within you a desire to become acquainted with your ancestors. The family members who preceded you have carved a pathway. The qualities you hold dear are a compilation of those who came before you. In this process of discovering and celebrating the lives of your ancestors, you will receive a

deeper love and appreciation for your heritage, have a better understanding of how you fit into it, and create a precious family heirloom for generations to come. Enjoy!

Laura Best

Table of Contents

General Instructions . . 8

"The day the big pine fell down." 1921

General Instructions

Heritage-type scrapbooking, in many ways, is more advanced than the scrapbook pages of modern day. For purposes of this book, the author is assuming that the reader has a working knowledge of basic scrapbooking supplies and techniques. If the reader is unfamiliar with scrapbooking, it is suggested that he reviews a beginning scrapbook volume before continuing with this book.

Supplies

When scrapbooking family history, a number of the traditional scrapbooking supplies and tools are used, such as decorative scissors, a crimper, stencils, stamps, an eyelet setter, permanent ink pens, and varied embellishments. Most other products on the market can be modified to work in a heritage forum. To stay authentic to the period, some modifications are necessary in a heritage album. For example, the chalk used is almost exclusively black or brown.

Supplies essential to family history scrapbooking include: archival spray, distressing materials, staining materials, and distressing tools such as sandpaper and wire brushes. As you advance in your designs and further your research, you may choose to add more supplies such as melting wax, a leather burner, and a metal engraver.

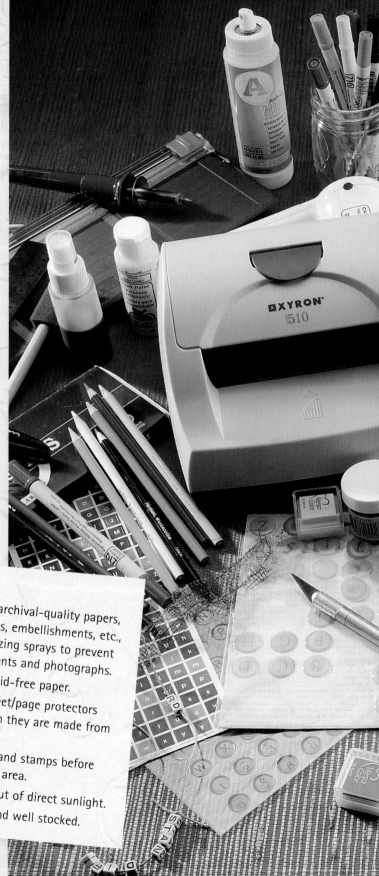

Tips:
- Be certain to use only archival-quality papers, albums, adhesives, tapes, embellishments, etc., as well as acid-neutralizing sprays to prevent deterioration of documents and photographs.
- Make photocopies on acid-free paper.
- When using "plastic" sheet/page protectors and sleeves, make certain they are made from acid-free polypropylene.
- Clean residue from tools and stamps before storing in a dry, dust-free area.
- Store tools and supplies out of direct sunlight.
- Keep supplies organized and well stocked.

Colors

Family history scrapbook supplies should have a distinctive color palette. You can certainly use more than the obvious black and brown hues; however, protect the integrity of the album by choosing colors that would have been available at the time period you are documenting.

Different background colors will bring out different tones and highlights in the photographs, documents, or mementos. Try several colors of paper until you find the one that complements the focal point of the photographs.

Muted yellows and greens are appropriate heritage colors and bring a soft look to a layout.

Tip:
Traditional heritage colors include earthy tones such as:

- beige
- black
- chestnut brown
- dark blue
- deep burgundy
- gray
- olive green
- rust
- tan

Colors not normally associated with, but accurate to, any time period are:

- bronze
- gold
- silver

Recopying traditionally black-and-white photographs to sepia sometimes brings a softer, more pleasing look to a layout.

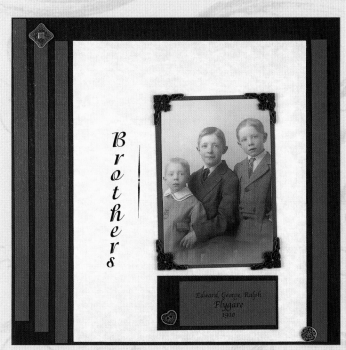

Regal dark colors make the photograph more formal and stately.

Monochromatic-colored papers complement photographs in a scrapbook.

Tools

Rustic pages of the Old West or military events can be challenging when creating an appropriate title. The look needs to be dignified and representative of the events.

Aged wood and authentic metal are appropriate for the time and lend themselves to historic scrapbook design. Don't be afraid to use tools such as a metal engraver or a wood burner when creating a page title. They may bring a more authentic look to the design.

Wood Burner

A wood burner actually burns markings into the wood. Hold the burner at an angle as you would a pencil. Avoid pressing too hard while burning. Keep the pressure consistent as you work.

This tool can also be used to mark on leather. Regardless of the material, practice on a scrap piece before working on the project to determine the pressure and speed you desire.

Metal Engraver

A metal engraver produces small pulses on metal, leaving a clean line. Hold the engraver at an angle as you would a pencil. Avoid pressing too hard while engraving. Keep the pressure consistent as you work.

Richardson

Sealing Wax

Sealing wax adds dimension and color to a design, while helping to keep ribbons taut and secure, avoiding glue or tape showing through. Either use melting wax and a stamp as you would find in a stationery store, or apply a bit of hot glue to the surface and add a bit of food coloring to tint.

I received the photographs and information about these family members from a lady I met in the cemetery I was visiting on Memorial Day. These images and part of the family had been missing from my records until then. After I designed this page of the family members, I included the complete story in the key.

Found Materials

Finding page accents and embellishments can be challenging, especially the further back your subjects go in history. Avoid limiting yourself to the traditional scrapbooking supplies.

This layout incorporates an actual T-shirt because it was an important part of the story behind the photograph. The leather background for the title was appropriate to the type of men in the picture and their surroundings in the rural Arizona desert. The leather and T-shirt were treated with archival spray before adding them to the layout.

Tip:

An avid scrapbooker saves scraps from other projects and layouts. Family history scrapbooking is a perfect outlet to use such scraps.

Other sources for finding authentic-looking materials for layouts include:

- out-of-print history books containing maps and pictures
- estate sales and antique stores
- relatives who have collected and saved old greeting cards, playing cards, or cooking labels
- flea markets and craft fairs

This entire page was made from bits of materials from scrapbook pages used throughout this album.

Consider using articles shown in the photographs that are reminiscent of the time period. Not only does the clothing give specific hints as to the era, it also gives ideas for accents to use on your page. Create accents, borders, and backgrounds with scraps of fabric, lace, ribbon, buttons, handkerchiefs, or swatches of old tablecloths or upholstery that are true to the period.

Phoebe Louisa Richardson Miller, 1876–1958

Constance, Paul and Virginia Miller

Tip:

There is a wide variety of colors and textures available with ribbon. It is great as a flat design element for backgrounds and texture. A well-placed ribbon needs little else to accent a page.

Run a ribbon through a sticker-maker machine and adhere to cardstock to avoid the look of glue seeping through.

Collecting

Making a family history album out of stacks of documents, photographs, and memorabilia seems like a huge undertaking. If you stay focused and organized, it is not so overwhelming.

Collect and gather family history items into one location. This grouping will include heritage and current photographs, documents, and memorabilia. Remember these people were full of life. They told jokes, had embarrassing moments, raised families, had relationships with people in town, and wrote letters to family members whom they rarely saw. Putting yourself in their surroundings may be an inspiration to the layout and the information you choose to include in the album. This may also help you direct your source when collecting information.

Every family is different. The paths your ancestors followed and their lifestyles and experiences will determine the types of documents you will find about them. The more you familiarize yourself with your ancestors' activities and lifestyles, the easier it will be to find documents and items about their movements.

As you collect items, be certain to document them as best you can. Ask yourself questions such as:

• Who is in the photograph?
• When was the photograph taken?
• What was the document for?

Photographs were not a high priority, or may not be available, the further back in history you go. You may be fortunate and have a number of photos because your family were photographers or had the means to have portraits taken. However, most people will find that their heritage photographs are limited.

The photographs need not have people in them—pictures of old houses, automobiles, and towns will add to the historical interest of a family's history. Give your reader some personal information and some perspective on a time period. Browse through back issues of magazines, dated copies of social etiquette books, or other publications with illustrations from the time period you are scrapbooking. The publications of the day will give you a feel for color schemes that were popular in that day as well as the "in" fashions, hairdos, and tidbits of information to include in your layout.

Consider interviewing family members, friends, associations, and clubs to find out who is working on a project similar to yours.

Scrapbooks have been kept over the years in various forms. Search out and inquire if other family members have kept a scrapbook of sort. This will give you access to stories, pictures, and journaling information that may be of interest to you. You may even develop a bond and be able to work together with family members who are also interested in family history or scrapbooking. Visit and research places that were important to your family:

• places they lived
• schools they attended
• churches they attended

Visit libraries to find newspapers of your ancestors' day on microfilm/database. Photocopy the front pages of newspapers with important dates as well as the advertisements showing products and prices of that day for things such as food, clothing, household items, and cars to add to the layouts.

Organizing

After collecting stories, names, dates, locations, and photographs, it is time to get organized. Find a clean work area to spread out your finds.

Organizing in Themes

Unlike an old scrapbook in which the pictures were pasted to black paper and dated with a white pen, a family history scrapbook chronicles a planned theme such as a holiday tradition, a family occupation, or a memorable family event. A scrapbook is more meaningful when it is organized in an easy-to-follow manner and each page has a purpose.

Remind yourself of the reason for the album. Organize the documents and photographs into piles that support the album theme you have chosen. If the theme is family war heroes, gather all documents, pictures, and histories dealing with the various wars. Then separate the materials by wars, chronologically, or by families, depending upon your album focus. Keep the group manageable.

Some examples of other focus groups would be:
- the last four generations of your paternal side
- a history of the families who carved a community
- experiences of explorers or pioneers

Tips:

- Talk with parents, grandparents, and aunts and uncles about information they may have.
- Venture out into the community to historical societies and examine the collections they keep.
- Explore the Internet for Web sites that cater to the historical period you are working with.
- Rummage through the boxes in the attic and basement.

Your findings may include:
- awards, citations, and achievement records
- birth, marriage, or death certificates
- family Bible
- finance ledgers
- journals and histories
- military records
- newspaper articles
- personal letters
- photographs, tintypes, postcards
- titles/deeds to property

Keep in mind that a family history scrapbook is a work in progress. It may help organize the page to collect in an acid-free plastic sleeve the photographs, embellishments, fibers, eyelets, sayings, and facts to be used. Recopy photos in sepia. Find specific dates for when the photograph was taken.

When enough of the page is assembled, you can more easily design the page. If photographs are not available, the page may be filled with text and embellishments. This type of page may also lend itself to memorabilia appropriate for the day, such as:

• brochures

• postcards

• ticket stubs

• food/clothing labels

If there are numerous pictures of the same event, choose the ones that are in the best condition and that tell the story of your ancestors accurately.

Once a page is completed, store the page in an acid-free plastic page protector.

Photographs should not be allowed to rub against each other. Also, embellishments that adorn a page should have no contact with surrounding pages. If you choose to not use page protectors, consider placing photographs on every other page to keep the designs from rubbing against one another.

Tip:
If you are missing something, attach a note about what is lacking, such as "Find the picture of Aunt Ruby with Uncle Frank" or "Find clip art of the Statue of Liberty."

Techniques

Deacidfying

Pay special attention to original items if combining materials in a family history scrapbook. Due to the acidity in papers, documents, newsprint, and books printed on poor-quality paper, all are prone to deterioration over time.

The poorest quality of paper is usually found in newsprint and tends to deteriorate rapidly—turning brown and brittle. Acid migration occurs when a low-quality paper bleeds onto neighboring pieces of paper.

Some old letters, invitations, and documents may have brown spots and stains where acid migration has already occurred.

The better the quality of the paper, the less acid migration you will see. The best solution is to photocopy the information onto acid-free buffered paper. Then scrapbook with the photo-copy only.

If you choose to include an original document—other than a photograph—such as a graduation announcement or a birthday card from your grandmother, use an acid-neutralizing archival preservation mist to deacidify the paper.

Mist papers, stamps, and newsprint with archival spray before adhering. Spray both sides of the paper to protect the paper from deterioration and crumbling for hundreds of years.

Tips:
- Text cut from books is often not archival-safe and should be sprayed.
- Archival spray should not be used on photographs.

Distressing Techniques

Adding an aged, weathered look to the background and design papers used in your layout will bring a more authentic feel to the project. Depending on the desired look, a number of techniques can be used to age your papers. Tearing, chalking, burning, sanding, and staining each bring a different element to your paper. A combination of techniques again brings another element of aging.

Tearing the paper toward you with your left hand leaves a white edge on the right-hand torn edge.

Tearing

Tearing paper of all textures and thicknesses offers a decorative edge that softens a page's look or makes it look more rustic. Vary the direction, speed, and angle of the tear to achieve surprising and spontaneous results.

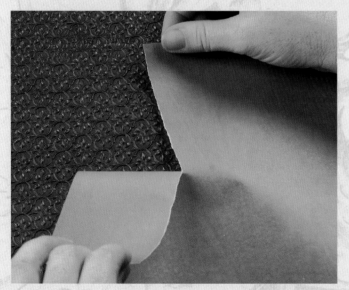

Tearing the paper toward you with your right hand leaves a colored edge on the right-hand edge.

Tearing vellum with the grain of the paper produces a fairly straight edge.

Chalking

Chalking can be used on all types of papers. This technique is used to antique paper, color edges of torn papers, add color to journaling blocks, add highlights and dimension, and shade diecuts.

To give a rustic look, shade photo edges with brown or black chalk. You can also crumple the photograph and rub over the picture with permanent dye ink.

Burning

Burning brings a distressed, weathered look.

Chalk tools include a sponge applicator, cosmetic sponge or cotton swab, and a protected surface.

Touch a piece of paper or cardstock to a flame just long enough for the paper to be burned. Keep the flame in control by blowing it out before it burns more than desired. If the paper has been ripped, the thinner part of the paper will burn more quickly.

Using an applicator, apply desired colored chalk to the edges of torn paper or vellum. You may substitute any nonoily, powder-based eye shadow or blush for chalk if desired.

Be aware that vellum catches fire quicker than paper, tends to melt, and burns inward rather that along the edges. The more inward you allow it to burn, the more fragile the vellum becomes. Too far in, and the burned area will tend to crack when cooled.

Sanding

Sanding photographs exposes the layers underneath the surface, leaving an aged well-worn look. While this technique is not suited for every photograph and certainly not for originals, it can add a rustic look. Randomly sanding photographs adds power to spreads dealing with divorce and troubled times.

1. Carefully tear along all four edges of the photograph, creating a rough perimeter. Choose the sandpaper, steel wool, or sanding block grit, depending on the severity of the aging you desire.

2. Working on a protected surface, sand the torn edges. Work in varied directions until the desired effect is achieved. Once the edges are finished, complete the look by lightly sanding the entire image with an ultrafine-grit sanding block.

Staining

Staining produces an aged look. Experiment with coffee, tea, and walnut ink to find the color you desire for the project.

Make a strong cup of tea or coffee. Place a paper item to be stained directly into the mixture, then remove the item immediately and allow to dry on a protected surface. Ribbon, lace, and fabric may need to soak for up to an hour for the color to stain the fibers. The longer it sits, the darker the material will stain. Allow the material to dry overnight. The item may be ironed flat with a dry hot iron.

2. Place the item to be antiqued on a protected surface and spray with ink. Using a sponge, dab ink to get the desired effect. The longer you leave the ink on an area, the darker it will become.

3. Sponge off any excess and leave to dry overnight.

1. Mix walnut ink powder in a spray bottle with water.

Note: Tea produces a yellow look, while coffee maintains a brown color.

Photographs

Photographs are the basic drive for a scrapbook. They give the best view into someone's life. Protecting photographs is one of the most important steps in scrapbooking and maintaining family history information.

Removing Photographs

If your old photographs were saved in a self-adhesive album, they should be removed immediately. If photographs do not come up easily, they may have already begun bonding with the adhesive.

Try one of the following methods for releasing photographs from albums:

- Use a thin craft spatula to pry up old photographs.

- Use a warm blow dryer to melt the gum between the photograph and the page.

- Run waxed dental floss between the photograph and the page.

- As a last resort, cut the photographs out of the album.

Repairing Photograph Damage

Old photographs may have deterioration or visual damage. Some minimal restoration can be done using a basic photo-editing software program on a home computer. Scan the photograph into the system, and use the software to remove stains and correct colors.

If there is more significant damage such as cracks, tears, or scratches, don't be tempted to restore them on your own. Find a photograph processor that offers digital restoration. Professional labs often have special cameras that allow them to photograph a picture and create a new negative. While creating the negative, the technician can add contrast to faded areas and lighten stains.

Photograph Care

Many of the photographs you are working with are probably "one-of-a-kind." To preserve original photographs, make copies on a high-quality color photocopier. Any subsequent copies should then be made from the high-quality copy, protecting the integrity of the original. Have black-and-white photographs copied on a color photocopier set in color mode for a richer look.

Delbert & Dorothy
Tobiasson
Logandale, Nevada   Circa 1939

Tip:

If this story had not been recorded, no one would know how such a picture came to be. Ask around to find out the reason behind the different photographs you find.

This couple was approached at their farm by a traveling photographer who asked to take their picture as they worked in their field. They stopped, posed, and went on with their day working in the field.

Photographic Occasion

Historically photographs were taken for a specific reason, such as a wedding or a civic event. However, photographers on occasion would go on the road to drum up business from people as they traveled.

love (luv) n. affection; strong liking:

gen'er a'tions descent 2 generations people born

joy

happy

Daddy

A JOURNEY of 1,000 miles BEGINS WITH one step.

happy travel

Tip:
Some modern premade embell-ishments can be altered to fit the era. Some can be adapted by replacing a color that is too bright or removing an object that would not have been available in the time period being represented. Generally, in family history scrapbooking, historical, western, or older embellishments can be used or adapted to the page.

Photographs in the nineteenth century were few and far between. A family group shot may have been taken for a special event, but it was rare to have a photograph of individuals or just a grandpa with his grandson.

When studying photographs, think about why the image would have been taken.
• Were they dressed up for a reason?
• Were they in the military?
• Was it a planned portrait?
• Was the family wealthy enough to have photographs taken often?

Scrapbooking without Photographs

Scrapbooks are associated with photo albums. However, unlike today when you can snap a picture at will or even stage a shot for a page you are working on, the people you are chronicling have most likely passed away. Therefore, you are limited to the photographs that were actually taken while they were alive and that are accessible to you. This will limit the pages you are able to put in your album; however, it does not mean you cannot feature a relative of whom you do not have a photograph. The documents we find about some ancestors may be the only record of them. Make a scrapbook page, with the documents or information you find being the focal point of the layout.

This layout was created without using any photographs. These ancestors lived before the time of photographs. I was, however, able to secure a hand-drawing of what they looked like and used it in the page layout as a decorative element to the story which showed the lifestyle of the day and type of relationship the couple had with each other.

Tip:

If you have no photographs, there are other options of documenting your ancestors:

- Draw a rendering of the people, house, or story you are sharing.
- Write the story of the ancestor in a creative way, such as with designed tags.
- Take a current photograph of the location, building, or event you are referring to.
- Check with local societies to see if a drawing or rendering of the event, building, or such is available for you to use.
- Draw a likeness of the person or place you are representing.
- Feature a found object from the person or event.

Unidentified Photographs

Photographs without the names, dates, and stories would soon become meaningless. So, for each photograph or set of related photographs you are not familiar with, ask yourself the following five Ws:

- Who is in the photograph?
- When was the photograph taken?
- Where was the photograph taken?
- Why was the moment significant?
- What are the people in the photograph doing?

Avoid referring to people in relation to oneself, such as "Great Aunt Claire, Mom, Dad, or Sis." Readers find themselves asking, "Whose Great Aunt Claire? Whose Mom and Dad?" Always use first and last names.

Remember that journaling isn't just for your own reference, but for future generations.

Tip:
If you can't identify anyone in the picture, you may want to assemble other photographs from that part of the family that you have identified. Look for similarities in the people and in the backgrounds.

Identify Photograph Subjects

Inevitably you will come across a photograph with people and events that you can't identify. Include a page in the album or design a frame you can add to your home decor dedicated to these photographs. Study the pictures with family members who look through the album. Ask family members questions such as:

- What is in the background?
- Where was the picture taken?
- Why was it taken?
- What were they doing?
- Who are they related to?
- Why do they look so happy or sad?
- Whose home is in the photo?
- Who in the family may know more?

Pay attention to details; for example, an American flag may only have 48 stars. Photographs such as this provide a good opportunity to include historical facts and remember the past in a fun yet personal way on the layout.

Once they have been identified, add the name, date, event, and location, then design a page about them to add to the album.

Take a framed photograph or an actual scrapbook page with you when you visit distance relatives, attend a family reunion, or even a family funeral. Inquire of family members who may know anything about photographs you cannot identify.

I was unsure about the girl in this photograph. I called the studio name stamped on the frame it is in. Though the name had changed, they were able to help me figure out what family she was from.

Tip:

Another way to determine who is in the photograph may be the type of picture itself.

- Daguerreotypes, ambrotypes, tintypes, and albumen prints are a few examples of older photographic processes that were used during past decades. By determining the type of photo, you can often estimate the time frame.

- If the picture was taken in a studio, many times the address of the studio is printed on the photograph or the frame it came in. Use city directories to find out when the studio was in existence at that address.

Use materials such as ribbon and lace that are appropriate for the time period or that explain the story told. Because of the elegant photograph, I added beadwork and vellum for a softer look.

Tip:

To add beaded wire strips, cut wire 1" longer than needed. Wire comes in different gauges; the higher the number, the thinner the wire. Bend ½" of one end at a 90-degree angle, then thread beads onto other end. When finished, bend ½" of other end. Pierce the paper with a needle and push the ½" ends of wire through, then bend to lay flat on back of page and secure with tape.

Cropping

Cropping a photograph means to cut a photograph or to place a frame around a photograph to improve the focus. In historic scrapbooking, the details that would normally be cropped out may actually help date the picture, such as the family car, the house, or an historical landmark. Don't crop historic photographs as you would current day images.

Be certain to include information about the items you kept in the picture when you journal.

Tips:

- Though cropping is a matter of preference, crop the photocopies only—don't touch the originals.

- Edges cut from decorative-edged scissors look better on mats than photographs (except for the deckle edges of white-bordered old photos.)

- Use simple shapes like ovals, rectangles, squares, or circles.

- Use sharp scissors to trim away unwanted background and objects in the picture.

- Keep cars, furniture, or other background images in historical photographs for era reference.

Storage

There are three main enemies to photographs: humidity, light, and temperature. Exposing photographs to any of these elements will speed up the deterioration process.

When handling old photographs and negatives, keep hands clean and oil-free. Oil and dirt can rub off fingers and onto the documents and photos, causing damage and deterioration. Using a pair of inexpensive cotton photography gloves will help keep fingerprints from causing long-term damage.

The less the originals are handled and exposed to light, the longer they are preserved. Creating duplicates of a heritage photograph allows you to share copies with your family. You can crop, enlarge, embellish, repair, and colorize on photocopies without the fear of destroying the original.

The older the photograph, and the more pertinent to historical events, the more interested clubs, associations, and historical societies are in old photographs. You may choose to make yourself high-quality photocopies, then donate the original photographs to a society.

Remove any negatives from the paper envelopes which come from a photo studio. The paper migration will eventually damage the negatives if they are left inside for an extended amount of time. Store negatives in plastic sleeves. Avoid placing them on top of one another to prevent scratching.

Tip:
Store all original photographs and documents as follows:
- in acid-free archival envelopes or photograph holders
- in a dark place with cool even temperatures
- away from acidic items—acid will migrate
- store paper unfolded and flat
- store albums upright
- deacidify newspaper articles and paper documents before storing in archival-safe sheet protectors. Or place documents between two sheets of black archival-safe paper, which can be replaced if acid migration occurs. Don't allow papers to rub against one another while stored.
- with labeled file dividers. These help to sort photographs into groups—by person, family, time period, life stages, or other groupings.

Tip:
The advantages to donating materials include:
- A society can professionally maintain the storage for you.
- The photograph is preserved in another location in the event that you lose or damage the copy you have.
- You may benefit from photographs that others have donate to the association you are doing researching with.

If you don't know your family's history, you are a leaf that doesn't know it is part of a tree.

— Michael Chrichton

Scrapbook Page Techniques

Guides

Some of the basic guides used in genealogy work can be designed to fit in your scrapbook. The addition of these guides will help explain the relationships between the family members in your album.

Family Tree

Once you have decided on the family group you will be featuring in your album, make some type of master document. I would suggest a typical family tree.

Complete this guide as accurately and as completely as possible. Do not guess. Once historical

information is printed and included in an album, it will lead others to believe it is factual. You may even forget which facts are true and which you guessed or estimated on.

Undoubtedly there will be missing information in your guide. You may come across this information as you work on your album. Make a list of resources that you can tap into for information:

• Which older relatives are still living?

• What books and historical sketches have been written on the family or the locations where they lived?

• What historical groups may have relevant information?

• Was a journal or family Bible kept?

MY FAMILY TREE

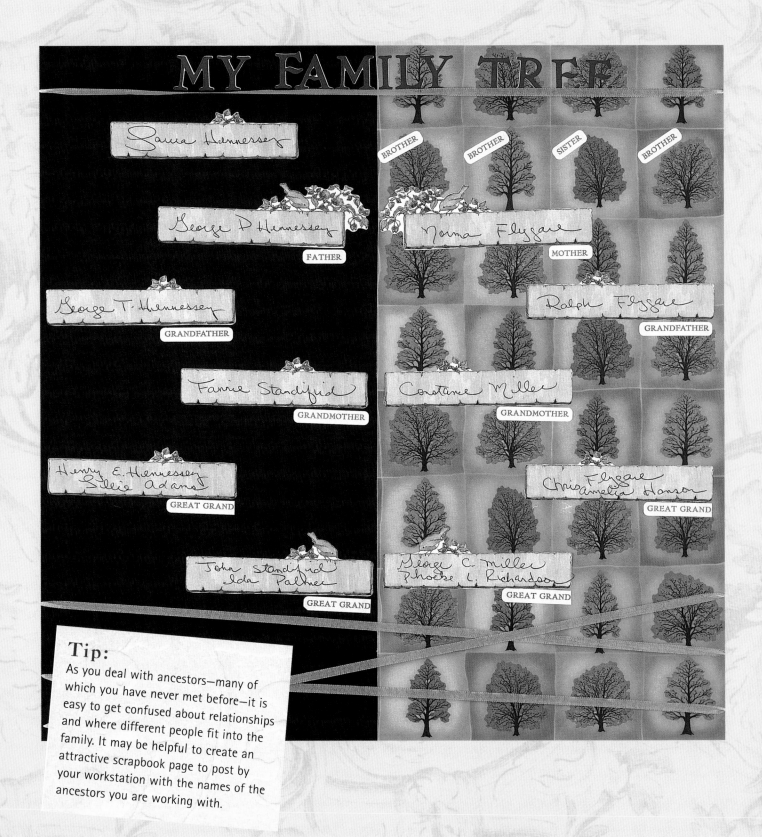

Sania Hennessey

George P Hennessey
FATHER

George T. Hennessey
GRANDFATHER

Fannie Standifird
GRANDMOTHER

Henry E. Hennessey
Sillie Adams
GREAT GRAND

John Standifird
Ida Palmer
GREAT GRAND

BROTHER   BROTHER   SISTER   BROTHER

Norma Flygare
MOTHER

Ralph Flygare
GRANDFATHER

Constance Miller
GRANDMOTHER

Chris Flygare
Chrisamelia Hanson
GREAT GRAND

George C. Miller
Phoebe L. Richardson
GREAT GRAND

Tip:

As you deal with ancestors—many of which you have never met before—it is easy to get confused about relationships and where different people fit into the family. It may be helpful to create an attractive scrapbook page to post by your workstation with the names of the ancestors you are working with.

Pedigree Chart

A pedigree chart is a diagram of your family tree, tracing your ancestry back through the generations. A written pedigree chart provides vital information including a full name; dates and places of birth, marriage, and death; as well as the relationship to other family members. A photograph pedigree chart puts a face with the names of your ancestors. This collection of ancestry photographs will become an heirloom for posterity.

Include a pedigree chart at the beginning of the album to show how the targeted group fits in the family tree. Keep these charts available while you work.

Tip:
Even if you do not have a photograph of your grandparents or great-grandparents it is still important to create a page whether it is written or photographs. Leave a blank space to add a photograph or the information when it does become available to you.

Journaling

One of the biggest struggles yet most important elements in family history scrapbooking is journaling. Because most photographs and materials are from generations ago, and include people you have most likely never met, everything you hear is secondhand.

Think of journaling as telling a story: write down the sort of things you say when you show someone your scrapbook or genealogy collection. Perhaps an ancestor was a privateer during the American Revolution, or a blacksmith who fashioned his wife's wedding ring himself out of gold he panned in the Black Hills.

As an exercise in collecting information, cut a series of questions into strips and place them in a jar. Take a strip from the jar each day. Ponder the question and write your thoughts and answers to the question about yourself. Keep all your answers together. When the jar is empty, not only have you learned the types of questions you are searching for but you have recorded your own history, traits, hopes, fears, and life experiences.

Some examples of journaling questions would include:

- What was your favorite vacation?
- What home cures or old wives tales for hiccups, toothaches, earaches, arthritis, etc., did you use?
- What was the most serious illness or accident you had?
- What is the kindest thing anyone has ever done for you?
- Who is your best friend?
- Did you have a childhood hideout?
- How did your mother spend her time?
- What was a typical day in grammar school like?
- What was it like to get a Christmas tree as a child?
- What is the most exciting place you have ever been?
- Talk with parents, grandparents, and aunts and uncles about information they may have.
- What games did you play as a child?

Using the same types of questions in the journal jar, begin interviewing older family members about a wide variety of topics. Record their answers.

Using this same technique, carry a notebook with you to record your thoughts, ideas, questions, and theories about your ancestors whenever you research. These thoughts may help you in future searches. Questions you might write down could include:

- Where can I locate a photograph of this person?
- Why did they move there?
- Why is my grandmother's brother not in any of the family photographs?
- Why is my married great aunt living with her parents in the census?

Be inquisitive about the documents and photographs you find. Finding answers to obscure questions will take you to resources and information you may not have thought important before. This type of researching may eventually tell the full stories of your family.

What was the most wonderful thing that ever happened to you?

What was your greatest sorrow?

Describe your kindergarten.

Describe walking down main street of your home town.

What did you do in your free time?

Describe a favorite vacation

Describe a perfect day?

What was your first paying job?

PERSONAL HISTORY JAR

Open this jar and you will find,
Questions that won't boggle your mind.
Take one out the first hundred days of the year,
Keep a notebook handy and a pencil near.

Tell what you do and the places that you go,
It will be special for those that love you so,
Your personal history is started without fear,
You'll have a treasure you'll hold dear.

39

Album Key

A family history scrapbook not only preserves the vital information of older generations but also is a good place to share family stories, historical events, feelings, family folklore, and group values. Since a variety of people may look at the album, their interest levels will vary. Some may be interested in the detailed stories, while others simply want to know the relationship between people. A good solution is an album key. This section of the album contains detailed information about family members, events, and situations without interrupting the integrity and pleasing design of a layout page. The key can also be easily updated as more information becomes available without disturbing actual scrapbook pages.

Another major role of a key is to inspire. Since you have put so much time and effort into the album, you should consider yourself a professional and an authority on your ancestors' lives. Be certain the album communicates the purpose you had for the book. When you have completed or are closing an album, consider ending the book with a personal letter from you or a statement of your hopes and desires for the album.

Hennessey Scrapbook Information Key

Days Gone By

The photo taken in 1936 is George Thomas Hennessey holding his only son George Dwight, age 1 in front of their home in Winslow Arizona. The photo taken in 1938 is George Thomas with is only two children, Barbara and George. The photo taken in 1989 is George Dwight with his father George Thomas standing in front of George Thomas' trailer home in Holbrook, Arizona. (This trailer was situated in Barbara's backyard. Barbara cared for her father until his death in 1991. The photograph dated 1973 is George Dwight, his parents George Thomas and Fannie, and his grandfather Henry Edward. They are standing in front of the house Ed lived in until he burned in his home at age 98.

Ask yourself questions such as:

- Where did you acquire the information you have? You may need to return to the source for further information, clarification, or to get an additional copy.
- How can you verify the information you have?
- What family groups or societies are available that share your family ties?
- What historical societies and libraries carry historical information that may include your ancestors?
- How long did it take you to complete the album?
- Who was the album created for?
- Why did you start the album in the first place?
- Do you have any stories to share that you experienced while making the album?

Layout

Certain basic layout guidelines are important to follow when designing a strong, pleasing page. It may be helpful to invest in a purchased kit with step-by-step instructions for putting a design together until you feel comfortable on your own. These purchased kits were adapted to fit the theme chosen for the pictures used.

Show different generations enjoying similar likes, such as this love of dolls.

Tip:

Some premade kits lend themselves well to a heritage theme. Look for kits that have the colors you are using in your album. You can create your own title and embellishments to fit your concept. Don't introduce an element that is not authentic to the time period. Kit papers can be easily altered by using one of the Distressing Techniques found on pages 22–25.

her·it·age [her-] ·is·

Home is where the heart is

The key to the future is in the past.

Family Treasures

home
1 the place where one lives **2** the p[...] [...]n or reared **3** a p[...] [...]g[...] [...] as home **4** a household [...] its affairs **5** an institution for orpha[...]

together

memories

unity

Family

[...]mily *n.* kin, folk, [...] [...]elations, tribe, [...] [...]ouse, kith and kin, [...]
family
[...] [...]ring [...] [...]race [...]ree, [...] [...]es [...]xtraction, [...] [...]nship, lineage, [...] [...]nd blood, strain

1 a gro[...] homegrown [...]eveloping in size, etc. *b)* the [...]

eft [...] an lega·cy

When you design layout ideas of your own without a kit, plan it out in your head to get an idea of what you are trying to portray. The presentation can be simple and elegant or complicated and busy. Consider the photographs, the events, and the people when determining the look of the layout.

Tip:
Without any journaling of personal information about this group the message of family is obvious. A key traditionally in scrapbooking means to unlock or the giving of permission to be intimate, which to many is what family is all about.

Fannie Standifird

When designing pages, pay attention to the various colors, textures, and patterns in the photographs used. Experiment with a variety of color combinations. Add rustic embellishments which are appropriate for the era. Include type fonts that accurately capture the time period.

Let the subjects in the photographs determine how simple or complex the look should be.

When working with a large family group photograph, remember it is a group of personalities with varying interests and accomplishments. It may help to ask yourself questions such as the following in determining how "busy" to make a layout to describe this diversity.

- What were the favorite memories of the family?
- What were the relationships like with each other?
- What did each end up doing with their life?
- Which person had special meaning to you?
- Which ones have you met? What was your experience?

Arrange the Page

The layouts throughout this book have been prepared on 12" x 12" paper; however, they can be adapted to an 8½" x 11" format or the size of your choosing.

Begin by experimenting with possible layouts for the photographs and memorabilia. Choose a number of photos that relate to a single theme, e.g. great-grandma's wedding. When you have the option, use only the photographs that are clear, focused, and best tell the story. If all you have is a poor copy or out-of-focus photograph, try creative ways to still show the image. Continue to look for better copies, then replace them as you find them. Remember, this book is always a work in progress.

Arrange and rearrange until the layout satisfies you. Leave room for titles, journaling, and embellishments. When you are happy with the layout, attach photographs and memorabilia to the page, using acid-free adhesive or tape. Stay with one and no more than two types of adhesive on each page. Even if all products are acid-free, the combination of different chemicals can cause undesirable effects.

I found this photograph among my family's records, but I know nothing about the people or place in the picture. I created a scrapbook page centered around what I thought a trip to town may include in the 19th century. When I am able to identify the people, I will rearrange the elements to tell a more accurate story. Until I know the facts, I have preserved this photograph and made it available to other family members to look at, perhaps someone who may have the necessary information.

If the information you know about someone is limited, create a collecting pocket until you have enough to develop a complete sketch of them. As you research and study your family, bits of information may surface about this person. As they are found, collect them in the pocket until you have a completed idea of them. Then the page can be redesigned according to what you have uncovered.

Think about it:
- What pictures do you have with like backgrounds?
- What pictures did you receive at the same time?
- What memorabilia is accurate to the era?

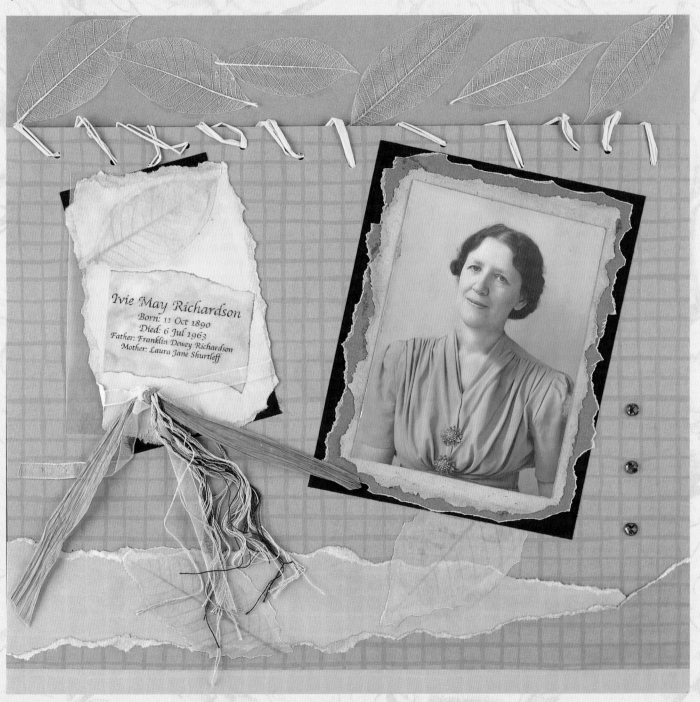

Ivie May Richardson
Born: 11 Oct 1890
Died: 6 Jul 1963
Father: Franklin Dewey Richardson
Mother: Laura Jane Shurtleff

Themes

A family history album does not necessarily mean you must do a complete story of all of your ancestors. Avoid being overwhelmed. Think smaller. Think in themes. A theme is an underlying subject that is common to the reason for the album. An everyday theme might be a family vacation, birthday parties, experiences at the lake, etc.

List the possible themes you can make from the information and materials you already have. Heritage themes can include:

- emigration or immigration
- holidays
- locations
- military
- nuclear family
- occupations

An album can consist of a single theme such as:

- ancestors who have inspired you
- family health issues
- family hobbies
- family pets
- family vacations
- grandparents
- holidays at the ranch
- involvement in news events
- treasures, heirlooms, collections
- tribute to a single family member
- favorite games or children's activities

Every album should include "firsts." The event does not have to be the first person to fly a plane or to be a famous dignitary. The first step of a child is just as important and very appropriate in a heritage scrapbook.

Tip:
Using techniques such as tearing, chalking, and coloring, even the most modern papers and embellishments can be used in a heritage album.

Tip:
For effect, keeping older photographs sepia and newer images in color makes a subtle statement about which photographs are more recent. To keep color photographs from over-shadowing sepia images, separate the two types of photographs on different pages.

The theme for these pages—which could later be expanded into an album— is "What did your family do for fun?" Additional information could be added to the album key including where your family liked to camp, the names and relationships of the people in the pho-tos. The location of the campouts and any notable experiences that happened during these outings.

Albums can be divided by groups:
- maternal or paternal family members
- pioneer ancestors
- family members in the armed services

The purpose of the album is not to show off what photographs you have found, but to document the history and lives of your ancestors. You may need to be creative on some ancestors where little photography or information is found. However, don't let these family members slip through the cracks without being recognized in some form.

SLEEP

When he is a little chap,
We call him
NAP.

When he somewhat
older grows,
We call him
DOZE.

When his age by
hours we number
We call him
SLUMBER.
— by John Tabb

Norma & Bobby
Hennessey

1958

Tip:
Apply a gold, silver, or colored pen to the edges of vellum or paper to link the color of the layout together and bring an added dimension to the page.

When developing themes, think about the story behind the photograph and the circumstances around the family at the time. The story behind this photograph was quite personal to the new mom in the picture. To honor the moment, a touching poem was added to the layout. The actual story is told in the key rather than on the page to preserve its personal nature.

Think about it:
- What intimate stories or events have happened in your family?
- What information is too intimate to share with the world yet should be remembered in your family?
- What spiritual experiences do you want to preserve?

General History

To put in perspective how your family fits into historical circumstances, research and list what was happening in the community, country, or world when someone in your family was born, got married, or was forced to move.

Your ancestors' social circumstances may have made a difference in the health, welfare, social, and occupational decisions they made.

Study area maps from your ancestors' day to determine the reason for relocating, or the reason for traveling over a certain route.

What events did your ancestors' experience or witness?

- Was it wartime or peacetime?
- What was being invented?
- What were people wearing?
- How many states were in the United States?
- What was the current mode of transportation?
- Who was president of the United States?

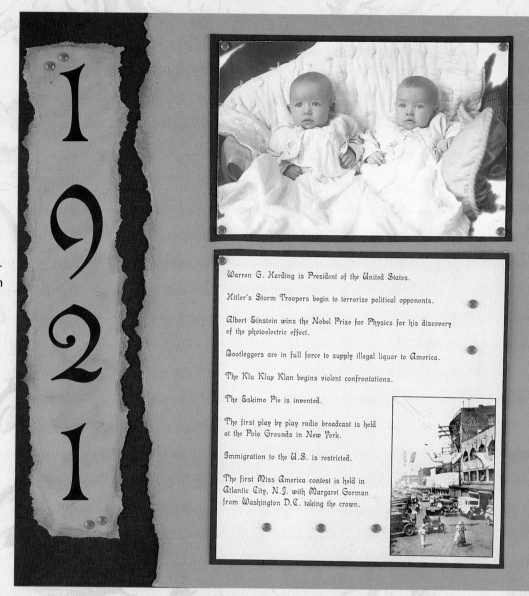

1921

Warren G. Harding is President of the United States.

Hitler's Storm Troopers begin to terrorize political opponents.

Albert Einstein wins the Nobel Prize for Physics for his discovery of the photoelectric effect.

Bootleggers are in full force to supply illegal liquor to America.

The Klu Klux Klan begins violent confrontations.

The Eskimo Pie is invented.

The first play by play radio broadcast is held at the Polo Grounds in New York.

Immigration to the U.S. is restricted.

The first Miss America contest is held in Atlantic City, N.J. with Margaret Gorman from Washington D.C. taking the crown.

Answers to these questions can be found by browsing the Internet or your local library about events of that day. Adding such information to your layout will add valuable details about the heritage and the history of the country. As a follow-up, it may be interesting to show what happened to these people later in their lifetime.

The innocent look on the faces of these twins reflects how little they knew about the world they were just born into. One of these twins, Jean, died of whooping cough at the age of three. The other twin, Arvin "Bud," lived until 1988.

Chronological

One advantage of a historical scrapbook is that you get to see how things turned out. How did the marriage turn out, how did the family survive the move, what did the children do when they grew up? A span of time can be chronologically represented in a single layout.

Think about it:

- How did your grandparents meet?
- How long had they known each other before marriage?
- What did courting in their day consist of?
- What were the conditions around their pending wedding?
- How did the extended families feel about each other?

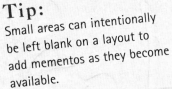

Tip:
Small areas can intentionally be left blank on a layout to add mementos as they become available.

One of the most inspirational events is the life span of a love affair. My grandparents met at college. My grandmother said that the day she saw my grandfather across the room, she knew they would be married. They were inseparable in life. After his death, she placed a fresh flower next to his picture every day.

These two pages represent the happiest and saddest days of Constance's life. Her wedding day was, in her word's "the highlight," and the death of her husband at the age of fifty was devastating. Looking at these layouts, nothing more needs to be said. The reader understands the meaning of the titles, without further words.

Think about it:

- What is the happiest or saddest thing you have had to deal with in your lifetime?
- What experiences or events changed the path of your family?
- What death in your family has been difficult for people to get over?
- What was a particularly happy time in your family's life?
- What event went from happy to sad or sad to happy in your family?

Tip:

When organizing thoughts and themes for an album, obvious groupings such as the birth and death of a person or the marriage and wedding anniversary of a couple can be treated as a set. Showing the circle of events builds a family foundation.

When designing pages representing chronological events, keep the photographs balanced. Because photographic technology has advanced, more brilliant photographs were available in later decades. To keep photographs equal in importance, change colored photographs to match the black-and-white or sepia photographs you are using from earlier years.

Think about it:

- How is the relationship between siblings in your family?
- If it is good, how does is stay strong?
- If it is strained, what caused the friction?

Tip:

When you design a relationship-themed page then repeat the concept with a later generation, a subliminal message is sent about the similarities of family ties which carry through the years.

Next to each photograph is a quote that each girl is remembered for saying as a toddler.

These sisters wanted to stay true to form with their photograph from their childhood and purposely took the same pose decades later to show that their friendship has not changed.

Tip:

The use of beads brings a subtle sparkle to a page. Be careful to not use beads that overpower the rest of the page by their size or color. They are embellishments, not the main focus.

Sisters

No friendship can quite compare to the special bond that sisters share...

Chance made us sisters, hearts made us friends

Norma & Carole Flygare

Special friends tied with heart strings

Sisters make the best friends

Tip:

When organizing page themes remember this is a chronicle of a family. It is an interesting comparison to show the same people and their relationship with each other through the years. It is also interesting to see how they have changed in appearance over the years.

A sister is a friend forever

It is interesting to see a number of generations pictured together. Here, the family comes alive. If you don't have a group shot of generations together, photographs of individuals work just as well. Another idea would be to show each generation individually but all at approximately the same age, so the resemblances are more obvious.

Think about it:

- What pictures are available showing more than one generation in your family?

- If you have no generation pictures with your immediate family, what cousins or aunts and uncles may have generation pictures?

- What individual pictures of different generations can you assemble?

Tip:
Record the relationships between a group of people in the key to protect the integrity of the page design.

The Hennessey Men

Henry Ed
1875-1975

George Thomas
1909-1991

George Dwight
1935-

Robert Wayne
1958-

Steven Lee
1962-

Evan Patrick
1979-

Mason
2004-

KATHERINE KINGDON 1981-

JULIE GILLETTE KINGDON 1956-

MARY FLYGARE GILLETTE 1928-

CONSTANCE MILLER FLYGARE 1903-1992

PHOEBE RICHARDSON MILLER 1876-1958

LAURA SHURTLIFF RICHARDSON 1858-1939

PHOEBE CHILD RICHARDSON 1832-1917

Each picture in this layout features the eldest daughter of each generation. Boxes were intentionally kept blank for Julie to add another picture when Katherine has her first daughter—adding another generation to this page.

Tip:

Bolder, more colorful papers can be used in heritage scrapbooking when you choose to send a specific message. Blues and lavenders may not be traditionally associated with heritage; however, they leave a feminine feel when only women are featured and especially when women of the current generation are included.

Ralph
Mary
Grant
Althea
Norma
Carole
David

Tip:

When displaying chronological photographs, document the date, occasion, event, and the names and relationships of the people. You may want to note how the relationship between these people has changed over the years.

Think about it:

- Have these siblings stayed close?
- Do they live by one another?
- Do they get together often?
- How have their lives turned out similarly? differently?

Memories of HOME

Tip:

When working with a chronological format, it is common to list all the individuals in the photographs. However, it may be entertaining for the viewer to test his knowledge of who is who in the photographs. It is important when developing a chronological page, that all the siblings are represented. After the viewer makes his guess, he can refer to the key to check his answers.

FLYGARE

When doing a family history album, emphasis is traditionally on the grandparents and great-grandparents. To complete the family experience, it is helpful to acknowledge the siblings of your grandparents as well. It is comforting for grandchildren to know that their grandparents stayed close with their siblings throughout their lives. This can be an encouragement for the relationship between children and their siblings today.

Think about it:

- Did your grandparents' siblings remain close?
- Did you meet any of them?
- Have you or your parents kept in touch with aunts, uncles, and cousins?
- What experiences do you remember about these people?

Fashion

Fashion has developed constantly through the generations. Sometimes the clothing worn was for practical reasons, sometimes it was just for attention or to show how well-off a family was. As you look through old photographs, you can often tell not only the era in which the photograph was taken because of the clothes that were worn, but you may be able to distinguish the financial well-being of the family, what their profession was, or where they were living.

The fad of wearing hats has changed over the decades along with what the hats looked like. This layout depicts a variety of hats, showing just such a change.

Tip:

Be certain to date the photographs in a layout of this nature, because fads do return again and could confuse the time period of the photograph.

Think about it:

- How did your ancestors dress?
- Could you tell their financial situation by their dress?
- Could you tell their occupation?
- Could you tell the time period or the where they were living by their attire?
- Do you own any attire from your ancestors?
- Is the fabric quite sturdy?

Over the years, it is interesting how products have changed, such as modes of transportation, electronics, children's furniture, toys, and fashion.

Showing something today and in the past will give the viewer a better perspective of how things have evolved over the years.

Change comes from necessity or progress. Explain in your journaling what has changed over time and why if you know the reasoning.

CRIBS & CARRIAGES

Think about it:

- What products today would your forefathers be amazed at?
- How has technology and transportation changed your family's lifestyle?
- Do you have any photographs of your ancestors working with old technology or transportation?

Tip:

Straight pins, safety pins, bobby pins, hat pins, all can be used for securing papers and photos together. Safety pins are an obvious choice for baby pages, while bobby pins go well with dressing up and small girls. Always avoid placing metal objects directly on photographs or documents as it will leave a rust mark. There are stickers and diecuts of various pins to use to protect the items on the page.

Emigration

Document the reason and circumstances of your family as they emigrated and traveled. It is interesting to see where families started. Remember the parents, at some point, met and married. Look into the emigration routes of all your family lines to get the complete emigration pattern. Put yourself in their shoes and describe what it would be like to move to somewhere you knew nothing about.

Think about it:

- Why did your relatives come to America?
- How did they travel?
- Where did they emigrate from? Why?
- Have you visited their homeland?
- What was their experience like?

In 1868, Thomas Hennessey left home at age 12 and stowed away on a boat from England to America. His sister cried from the shore as she watched the ship sail away. Thomas never saw any of his family members again.

He never learned to read or write. His signature was simply an X.

Thomas became a rancher in Texas. In 1874, he married Matilda Martin in Texas. They had 10 children before they divorced in 1902. He lived until he was 71 years old.

Tip:

Look for patterned papers that complement the story of your layout. You may need to distress the paper in some manner to age it for the time period.

In the nineteenth century, extended families tended to live by one another. When they emigrated, they moved as a group. They may have traveled at different times, but eventually ended up in the same community. Sometimes family members lived with extended family due to the various chores and cares that needed to be handled. Following families through a census record may show this type of information. Be cautious as you read the records. The census taker may have asked who lived there; but if cousin Joe was visiting for the day or week, they may report him as well. Don't confuse him as a member of that direct family.

When you look through census records, be certain to look at the neighbors as well. Neighbors tended to emigrate with them. You may find a group of families emigrating and living by one another for a number of years.

To give the reader a glimpse of the area, you may want to include a photograph of what the area looks like today. You may be able to locate a photograph of the residence then, or you may want to include a map from an atlas of the time and mark approximately where they lived.

Be certain to include a brief biography of the family. Use a photocopy of the census record; it will show the address, who was living in the home, and the neighbors.

Tip:

Create a page dedicated to the concept of taking the census. Depending upon the year, the census may state where your ancestor originated from, where he was born, who he married, his children's names and ages, and his occupation.

Think about it:

- Where were your family members living before they came to the United States?
- Did they travel with extended family?
- Did they homestead?

Using the census, follow the travel patterns of your family. When they do not show up in the next census, find them. Look at what was going on historically in their part of the world to make them move? If someone is missing, they may have stayed behind or got married and are now under a different name. These questions can be answered by looking at vital records such as death and marriage records.

Document the reason and circumstances of your family's movement. It is interesting to see where families started and ended.

Ed and Lillie Hennessey moved with their children Leola and George from Texas to Arizona in 1911. Ed traded their Texas home for a covered wagon with a chuckbox on the back. He harnessed his two plow horses Dick and Frank to the wagon. Lillie supplied the wagon with cast iron Dutch ovens, bedding, clothes and an organ.

While the family crossed the hot desert a man in a buggy came by and said, "You're never going to make it." But Ed replied "You don't know these horses."

The children walked behind the wagon in the deep sandy ruts. When they camped for the night Ed tied the horses to the wagon and gave them grain and water. He was afraid the Indians would steal the horses in the night so he stayed up through the night.

The family settled in Holbrook, Arizona, where Ed found ranching more to his liking than farming.

Their home was next to the railroad tracks. When the Holbrook to Gallup train passed by, the crew would blow the whistle and throw off ice for the kids. When the weather was cold, they would throw off chunks of coal.

TEXAS BOUND

Tip:
A wide variety of miniature objects can be found throughout craft shops, such as these small metal serving spoons, which could have been found in the "kitchen" at the end of this covered wagon.

Think about it:
- Did the move make life easier or harder for them?
- Were they excited? scared? anxious?
- How did they travel?
- Did they travel in a group?
- What was their experience like?
- Do you still have family living there today?

Seasons

The seasons were important to your ancestors because they may have depended heavily on the weather for their crops and work activities. It was not uncommon for a celebration to be centered around the changing of a season.

Whether there was a house-raising project in the spring after a long winter or after harvesting in the fall, many neighbors and family assembled to help one another with their chores and needs. These may not have been documented with photographs, but the stories can still be told in a creative way.

Depending on the line of work and the area of the country in which one was living, seasons played a big part in what they did on a daily basis, and in their survival.

Constance's favorite season was Spring. She spent her free time walking through the fields by her farm, picking flowers.

Tip:

When properly pressed and dried flat, leaves and flowers complement scrapbook pages beautifully. To protect the papers and photographs, use special acid-free pockets, or make your own protective coverings from page protectors. Don't hesitate to use any number of natural accents such as twigs, rocks, or dried leaves. Just be cautious of the direct contact with the photographs and important documents.

Think about it:

- How did the seasons affect your ancestors?

- What did each season mean to your ancestors?

- Some professions work seasonally. How did they survive the rest of the year?

- Did the season matter to your ancestors' livelihood, such as planting crops?

- Which season was your relatives' favorite? Why?

- Was there any special celebration aside from the obvious holidays centered around the seasons?

Spring

Spring festivals are often celebrated, marking the end of a harsh winter. The arrival of new plants and the lengthening of days was very important to earlier societies. Spring festivals originated from the celebration of the birth of farm animals and the growth of new crops.

Think about it:

- What did your family celebrate in the springtime?
- What is your favorite childhood spring memory?
- What seasonal family events have turned into traditional activities?
- Which generation did they start with?
- Have you carried them on with your family?

Tip:

If you do not have a photograph of the actual event, take a picture of the outcome. In this case a photograph of your current family enjoying a huckleberry pie next to the recipe of your family shows the same story.

Growing up in the northern parts of Montana, we commonly went on family ventures in the springtime to pick huckleberries. Though most of the berries never made it into the baskets, we came home quite full. We bottled the huckleberries for the winter, but reserved enough to make a cherished huckleberry pie. This was a treasured family annual event.

Summer

Even though most summer festivals celebrate historical events, the actual summer months are associated with relaxation and vacation.

As you research your family, be aware that the further back in time you go, the less the likelihood that the family actually went on vacations.

Tip:
Letter stickers do not need to be peeled away from the paper. Sometimes the white background is needed so the letters do not get lost in the layout.

Tip:
When using stamps, either use the complete stamp or tape off parts to use only a portion of the stamp.

Think about it:

- What did the summer mean to your family?
- What did they do as children in the summertime?
- Did they have chores or a job?
- Did they travel or stay at grandma's?
- Did they have family vacations?
- Did they attend a youth or sports camp?
- Did they go to the lake, the mountains, or the beach?
- Did they enjoy the summertime?

As I looked through old photographs, I found that my mother and grandmother both had a pool or a pond by their home; and spent their leisure time by the water.

65

Legacy

Heritage

Constance, Ralph & Mary Hygare

My Family Tree

Autumn

Autumn is a period of dying, as the summer ends, and a time to harvest. A number of festivals are celebrated dealing with the harvest and the changing weather. As you research, you may find that the fall was a busy time. The daylight hours were short and the chores of preserving and preparing for the winter was upon them.

Think about it:

- What did the fall mean to your family?
- What were their chores like?
- Did they harvest crops?
- Did they have a large garden?
- Did they preserve foods or have a root cellar?
- What did they do for fun in the fall?
- Did they participate in hayrides, bonfires, and festivals?
- What changes were made when the days became shorter?

Tip:
Though traditionally heritage photograph shapes are oval and rectangle, this rule can be broken to blend the photographs with the page theme.

Winter

As the darkest, coldest season of the year, winter to many is a depressing time. For my ancestors in the winter, food was scarce, socialization was almost nonexistent, and the day's chore was keeping the house warm and comfortable.

Tip:

When one photograph is too dominant for the rest of the page, cover it with a bit of vellum to tone it down.

Think about it:

- Did your family store food for the winter?
- Did they have chores such as chopping wood and keeping the fires lit?
- What was the light source when it got dark?
- What did they do at night once the sun was down?
- Did they go to bed early and arise early?
- What were the biggest hardships?
- What fond memories do you know?
- Did they ski? ice skate? camp in the snow? hunt?

Tip:

To add extra dimension and interest to photographs, cut them apart. Separate the pieces, then reassemble and glue them onto a mat, leaving a little space between the pieces.

The photographs in this layout were color-copied with an intensional blue tint to represent how cold the children were.

Holidays

The majority of documented memories and traditions are centered around holidays. Family gatherings at holidays and festive times are common; however, the traditions of simple things are lost when they are not documented.

Through the years, holidays and festivals have evolved. Some festivals have combined to make up the current holidays and celebrations we honor today.

One thing constant with holidays is the gathering of family. In many instances, holidays are the only times families get together, and often the only times photographs are taken of the family as a group. While celebrating these events, memories and traditions have developed and usually are handed down through the generations.

Through interviewing older family members and studying historical events, discover where the traditions you cherish originated from.

Try to find memorabilia and photographs of how your relatives interacted and celebrated with each other. As you study family holiday photographs, jot down your feelings of what the various holidays and traditions mean to your family.

This man asked his bride-to-be to marry him by sending this valentine through the mail. A photocopy of the actual valentine and envelope were used in this layout to protect the original document.

Think about it:

- How was each holiday celebrated in your grandparents' or great-grandparents' day?
- What traditions have stayed constant and what activities have changed?
- What do you do differently than your grandparents?
- How are present and past traditions tied together?
- What did each holiday mean to your ancestors?
- Did your ancestors bring traditions from their homeland?
- Does your family follow them today?
- Do they mean the same to your family today?
- Does a holiday celebration prompt an emotion?

Valentine's Day

A lighthearted holiday is traditionally a time when people express feelings of friendship, affection, and love. Inevitably there are struggles in a family, so it is important to capture the romantic, happy aspects of your heritage to celebrate the tender relationships in your family. This can be expressed with a story of a proposal or romantic moment.

Think about it:

- What couples in your family have been sweethearts for years?
- Has anything special happened in your family on Valentine's Day?
- What was the best valentine you ever received?
- How did you celebrate at school?
- Did you exchange cards with family members or neighbors?
- Did you do anything differently at home than on any other day of the week?
- Did you observe valentine-type celebrations at other times of the year?

Tip:

If a couple divorces, there will most likely be no photographs of them together later in life. If possible, extract the couple out of a family group photograph taken at a family event such as a wedding to show how they looked in their later years.

Fannie divorced George after 17 years of marriage because he was an alcoholic. She remarried Lee Thompson. After 14 years of marriage, Lee was killed by a drunk driver. Fannie was devastated. Though she had divorced George 15 years earlier, they spent the last few years of their lives living next to each other—always remaining close friends.

Of course you may be bashful
But think how much 'twould please me
If you would be my valentine
And try no more to tease me.

Birthday

In ancient societies, life was hard and survival to old age was rare. Every year of life was a triumph over death, so birthday anniversaries were joyously celebrated. In some societies, gifts are offered by the birthday honoree as his appreciation of life.

Tip:
When a photograph was obviously taken during a specific season, follow the theme such as including leaves with a photograph taken in autumn.

Aspen

Grandma Louisa's
6oth birthday
29 Oct 1876-
29 Oct 1936

Think about it:

- What were your family birthday celebrations like?
- What traditions are honored?
- Were there any surprise parties?
- What traditional foods were served?
- Were there any traditional birthday wishes? songs? games?
- Is there a traditional gift given?
- Do you recall any landmark birthday events such as 50, 75, or 100 years old?

LAURA

1964

As a child, I had a porcelain lamb figurine, which sat atop every one of my birthday cakes. I took a photograph of the lamb as it is today, to place next to a photograph of me as a child with the lamb on the cake.

Easter

Easter was originally a pagan festival, during which eggs were given as the symbols of new life. Festivals were held to celebrate the birth of farm animals and the growth of new crops.

Today many Christians celebrate the resurrection of Jesus Christ by attending a church service. My family traditionally received a new outfit to wear to church on Easter. We colored and hunted for Easter eggs and received a basket full of candy on Easter morning.

Think about it:

- What does Easter mean to your family?
- How did you celebrate?
- Did you observe Good Friday? the Passover? Palm Sunday?
- Did you get a new outfit? Who made it?
- Did you go to church?
- Did the Easter Bunny come to your house?
- Did you color and hide eggs?
- Did you participate in an egg-rolling contest?
- Did you have an Easter egg basket?
- Did you have traditional foods such as ham or lamb?
- What was your dinner like? Who was invited?

The photographs in this layout were cut in egg shapes to represent the hard-boiled eggs colored during the season. Removing the corners not only softens the shapes but subliminally goes with the seasonal symbol of birth and a new beginning.

Patriotic

Holidays which have derived from political or military events continue to be celebrated over the years. The meaning of each holiday has changed over the generations, depending upon peoples' experiences with war, freedom, and the country's economic status. Some generations have not gone through wartime; however, they still benefit from the freedoms gained at the expense of others and still celebrate at parades and picnics.

Think about it:
- Were any of your relatives involved in any major conflicts?
- What branch of the service were they in?
- What was their experience like?
- How long were they active?
- Was it their choice to serve, or were they drafted?
- Were they wounded? killed?
- Did Flag or Veteran's Day have a special meaning to someone in your family? Why?
- Did you have a traditional way to celebrate?

This layout was a tribute for a single family member and the wars and situations he was involved in. I dedicated a complete page to him because he served in a number of different wars.

A symbol represents an abstract idea, concept, or feeling. A familiar symbol in the United States is the American flag. Other symbol examples include the color purple, which stands for royalty; lions, which stand for courage; and the skull and cross-bones, which symbolize death.

These two pages represent two completely different eras. Notice how the children historically salute the flag and recite the Pledge of Allegiance in school. The other page shows the freedom to honor your country wherever you are.

Out of honor, these children saluted the flag each morning before dressing.

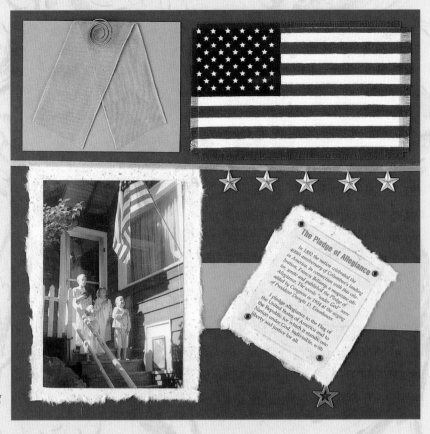

Think about it:

- Was your family patriotic? Why?
- What does the flag mean to your family?
- What experience has your family had with the flag or other patriotic symbol?
- What other symbols were important to your family in past generations?
- What symbols have carried through the generations?
- How have they shown respect for these symbols?

The old photograph of the class-room saluting the flag and the Pledge of Allegiance quote were taken from an old history book. The papers were deacidfied along with the cloth flag.

Halloween

The Halloween holiday has evolved over the years from being associated with evil times, such as witchcraft, to a celebration of trick-or-treating and dressing in costume.

An actual lasso-type rope was used in this layout to keep with the Halloween costume theme. The lasso was made of heavy material and secured with large glue dots.

Think about it:

- How did your family celebrate Halloween?
- What traditions did they observe?
- Did they bob for apples, attend a fall festival, or light a bonfire?
- Did they carve pumpkins or decorate their house?
- Did they dress in costume and go trick-or-treating?
- What types of costumes did they wear?
- Who made the costumes?
- How was the holiday celebrated at school?
- Did anyone play tricks?
- Were any scary stories traditionally told?

To make a fall page, the appliquéd leaves and acorns were salvaged from an old sweater found at a thrift shop. They were deacidified and adhered with glue dots.

Gobble 'til you Wobble

To Make a Turkey
by Katie Best age 7

1. Buy the biggest turkey you can find.
2. Take it home.
3. Keep it in the sink.
4. Stuff the tail with broken bread.
5. Put it in the stove until the house is too hot, maybe 10 minutes.
6. Take it out of the stove.
7. Find the wishbone.
8. Don't eat until after the prayer.
9. Have turkey all week.

1964

Potatoes & gravy. turkey & dressing. being with family is truly a blessing.

1978

1993

1998

Thanksgiving

Thanksgiving Day is a day of tradition. Whether it is who usually gets together, or the foods that are prepared from year to year, this holiday is for most a family day.

Think about it:

- What does Thanksgiving mean to your family?
- Do you have ancestors involved with the Pilgrims?
- What Thanksgiving traditions have been passed down?
- Which traditions do you maintain?
- Where did they begin?
- Who do you celebrate with?
- What does your family traditionally like to eat?
- Who cooks?
- Do you have a traditional activity such as taking turns expressing thanks for something, watching football, or playing board games?

Paper tearing can be adapted to all paper textures and colors. Tear paper into strips or shapes to resemble a turkey as was done here. When using this technique, tone down any bright-colored paper with chalk to stay consistent with the heritage colors of the rest of the album.

Tip:

Before television and movies, people relied on arts and crafts to fill their time. Consider some of the popular crafts of the day and incorporate them into your layouts. There are a myriad of needlework Christmas patterns on the market to choose from.

Christmas

Of all the holidays, Christmastime traditionally had photographs taken with extended family.

Think about it:

- What has Christmas meant to your family?
- What traditions are honored?
- Where did they begin?
- Who celebrated together?
- What did they eat?
- How did they spend Christmas day?
- What were the decorations like?

Tip:

When including family shots of a holiday event, do not crop out the detail. Include favorite pets, familiar furniture, and well-loved areas to evoke reminiscence of the time.

Tip:

When combining a number of generations in a layout, find a paper and embellishments that are suitable for each time period.

Tip:

Whenever different generations and decades are represented, be certain to document the dates the best you can.

Celebrated Events

Family Reunions

Family reunions are ideal occasions to have documented in a family history scrapbook. Here is the opportunity to identify and see a large number of relatives together. Instead of a lengthy listing of all the people at the reunion on the scrapbook page, put the bulk of this information in the key. On the layout page, give the bare facts such as the last name, the date, and the location. The title or headline will be the biggest giveaway that this is a reunion.

Think about it:

- Has a family member hosted a family reunion recently?
- Who sponsored the reunion?
- Where and when was it held?
- How often have they been held?
- What were the activities?
- How many people came?
- Was there anything special about the reunion?
- Is the address list still available?

Tip:
If you have regular family reunions, create an album of these events to hand down. Identify as many as possible in the photographs before this knowledge is gone. Ask older relatives, or people who may have been at the reunion, who everyone is and what the relationship is between the people.

To easily identify the people in a large group photograph, develop a system of marking each person. This example was drawn on a light-box with tracing paper placed directly over a the photograph. The people images were then numbered. This drawing was secured to the back of the layout page.

Tip:
Circulating a roster around at a family reunion gives participants the opportunity to update family members' names, give current addresses, and show any willingness to participate in family group projects.

Tip:
A family reunion is a perfect place to take a family history scrapbook. Let people look over the pages and reminisce about the stories. Listen to their comments. Have them reconfirm the dates, places, and names. Be prepared: they may want copies of photographs that you have. They may also comment on the fact that they have a better photograph or a different grouping of a family. Let them comment on the accuracy or inconsistencies, and maybe add information you are missing. Accept this information graciously.

Weddings

Depending on the era, weddings were celebrated in a different way. Unlike the huge wedding events of today, marriage ceremonies were not lengthy in preparation and did not require a special dress.

Tip:

When possible, use original items from the event being scrapbooked. Be certain to preserve found objects with archival spray and mounted with minimal archival adhesive.

Think about it:

- What was your parents' or grandparents' wedding day like?
- Who was there?
- What did they wear?
- Did the families know each other?
- Were there any family objections?
- Where did they get married?
- Was there a reception or celebration?
- What did they eat?

My maternal great-grandparents' wedding was not a big gala. They gathered with family for a small ceremony and spent one night away together. No pictures were taken. My parents, however, had their wedding written up in the newspaper, a huge reception, and a number of parties. The gloves, newspaper article, and invitation used in his layout are original.

Anniversaries

Wedding anniversaries have traditionally been treated as a celebration. Generations ago, people did not live as long as they do today, so it was a landmark to hit fifty years of marriage. Though people are living longer now, a fifty-year anniversary is still a milestone due to the rise in divorce. If you find a photograph of a wedding anniversary for your grandparents or great-grandparents, it most likely is a landmark one since photographs were not taken as liberally as they are today.

Think about it:

- Did your grandparents have an anniversary party?
- Was the celebration a surprise?
- How did they celebrate?
- Who was the host and who attended?
- How many grand- and great-grand-children did they have?
- How was their health at that time?
- Were they happily married?
- Any significant gifts, toasts, events?

Tip:
Ribbons, beads, and charms are all appropriate for anniversary layouts. Beads and charms can be threaded onto wire, sewn, or glued. To attach small beads, spray a ribbon with adhesive, then sprinkle beads on top. Gently press down to secure in place. Lift and gently shake paper to release any loose beads.

Folklore & Traditions

An important purpose of a family history album is to document the stories and traditions of a family.

Families who have listened to stories about the hardships of relatives who first settled the West, or who were on opposite sides of the Civil War, realize that if this information is not recorded in some manner, these stories soon become lost to future generations.

Traditions are the reflections of beliefs, superstitions, and personalities of a family.

Even families fragmented by geography, death, or divorce can establish a sense of belonging through family history albums.

Think about it:

- Were there any untraditional marriages in your family?
- What were the circumstances?
- Was there a feud or misunderstanding that took years to resolve?
- Was it ever settled?

This feud started with a shotgun wedding. The boy got his brother's sister-in-law pregnant. He was forced to marry her at gunpoint, then ran away. He was never found by the bride's family, and was finally buried in an unmarked grave not far from his hometown. The location of the grave stayed a secret among his family for years. The children of this family, especially the illegitimate child, were instructed not to talk about this event.

Tip:

If you have stories that are too touching or too personal to share with the casual viewer, consider one of the following:

- Write the details down, place paper in an envelope, and work the envelope into the layout.
- Write the story in the key.
- Create a photo flap. Use the card inside to journal the information.

Family Stories

Family stories can entertain, teach, and inspire family members for generations. Happy stories bring a quick smile or chuckle, while sad stories are shared to inspire others to carry on during hardship.

Happy Stories

Relating stories of family jokes through the generations brings ancestors to life and puts them in a light of being real and human.

Think about it:

- What family jokes or humorous stories do your family members share?
- Where did they begin and who was involved?
- What embarrassing moments have turned into a funny family story?

You call her "Duke?" We call her "Honey Grandma."

D u K e

Constance M. Flygare
Montana, 1971

Tip:
The complete story behind a joke can be written in the key for family members who do not know the joke.

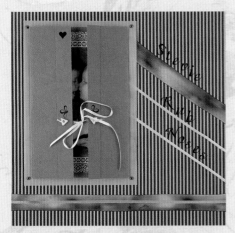

To add to the suspense of this joke, a covering is placed over the children to show how secret their joke was to them.

Remember that your ancestors laughed, sang, and joked just as you do. It is comforting to know they had fun and were able to laugh at and with each other.

Think about it:
- What funny story reveals the character of an ancestor?
- What were your relatives' senses of humor like?
- Did they joke around?

The words on this layout were hand-stitched on. Tissue paper was placed on the paper before stitching, then randomly pulled away, leaving some tissue paper for a more rugged look.

She is quiet

...but she carries a big stick!

Little boys are notorious for playing in the dirt. Showing activities, such as this, creates a bond with other generations which are involved in the same activity.

Think about it:
- What "messes" did your family members get into?
- Were they punished? How?
- Did their parents laugh it off?
- What was the discipline like in these families?
- Was a lesson taught?
- What did you do as a child that got you into the most trouble?
- How did your parents handle it?

A design element was subtly created by continuing the tire rut marks in the photograph onto the paper. This line draws the eye into the picture.

To subtly show dirty becoming clean, the paper, decorative envelopes, and chalk gradually went from brown to white, just as the boy became clean from dirty.

During Ed and Lillie Hennessey's first weeks of marriage, Ed was clearing a road to their home of sagebrush. Each day when he returned home he passed by a

P R A I R I E
D O G

mound. He thought it strange that the prairie dogs looked white in color. Years later, Ed learned that when Lillie made a batch of bread that did not turn out, she poured it down the prairie dog hole covering them with flour.

1 9 0 1

WHITINGTON CO.
FLOUR
100% PURE

Humorous stories bring ancestors to life. They did silly things, got embarrassed, and laughed. This human side gets forgotten over time.

Think about it:
- What were the best foods your grandma made?
- Was your grandmother good in the kitchen?
- Are there any humorous family stories to do with cooking?

Tip:
If you do not have a photograph of the family story you are sharing, find clip art or a character out of a coloring book. Color and embellish the image to match the layout design and the story.

My great-grandmother, as a new bride, made bread every day for her husband. Her husband thought it strange as he walked home from work, to see white prairie dogs, which is not the traditional color. Years later, it was confessed that whenever great-grandma would make a batch of bread that did not work out, she would dump it into a prairie dog hole to hide it.

Stories such as these little children and grandchildren in on the secret that their parents were once children too. Whether your parents fell asleep while waiting for dinner or stole the cake right from the oven, kids will be kids, regardless of the generation.

Think about it:

- What experiences do you recall happening in the kitchen?
- Were children allowed in the kitchen to learn or help?
- What were your ancestors' expectations at the supper table?
- What were your ancestors' responsibilities at meal times?

Tip:

Sometimes family stories and jokes are still told; however, the origin is forgotten. Find out and document the simple story behind precious photographs such as these. Daily occurrences bring ancestors more to life.

Sad Stories

Sad events that happen in a family should be documented as well as the happy things. This brings a better understanding of the lifestyle and trials, and gives a more accurate look into the lives of your ancestors. Life was not full of only fun and happy times. They had struggles as well; and not just the publicized ones such as crossing the plains or traveling on the Mayflower. Your ancestors had personal loss and sadness.

Think about it:

- What tragic events happened to your family?
- How was the incident handled?
- What damage did the event leave your family?
- How did the family members recover?
- What stories are told today about these incidents?

The only photograph with Reba in it was a group shot taken at a family reunion. I cropped out the rest of the people to focus on her and her husband.

Reba Kennington Miller was killed at the age of 24 when she was struck by **lightening** during a thunderstorm. The lightening bolt came through a window into the kitchen where Reba was visiting with her brother and sister-in-law in Thayne, Wyoming. She left behind two daughters ages 3 and 4. Her husband Frank Miller remarried and raised the girls. 8 Aug 1941

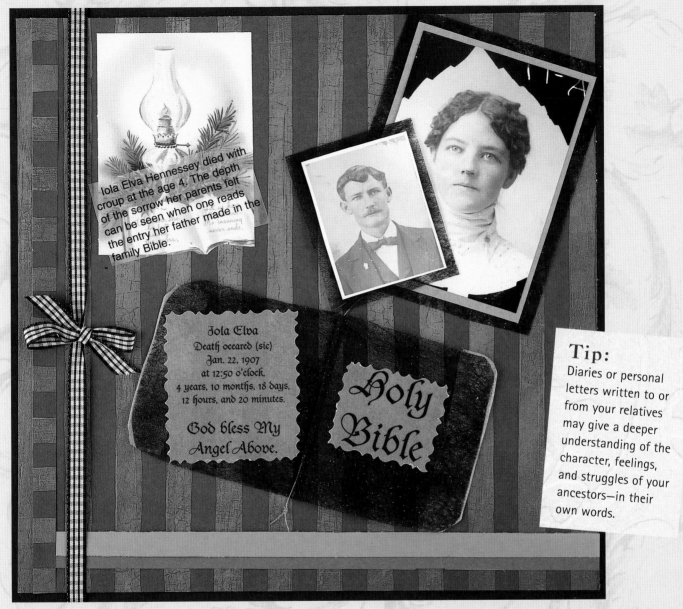

Iola Elva Hennessey died with croup at the age 4. The depth of the sorrow her parents felt can be seen when one reads the entry her father made in the family Bible.

Iola Elva
Death oceared (sic)
Jan. 22, 1907
at 12:50 o'clock,
4 years, 10 months, 18 days,
12 hours, and 20 minutes.

God bless My
Angel Above.

Holy Bible

Tip:
Diaries or personal letters written to or from your relatives may give a deeper understanding of the character, feelings, and struggles of your ancestors—in their own words.

Documenting how an ancestor felt about an incident brings them more to life. Without knowing their feelings, we can only assume they would react as we would. The personality and sensitivity of Ed losing his daughter is evident in the entry he made in the family Bible.

This family's four-year-old daughter died of the croup, devastating her parents.

Think about it:
- How did tragic events affect your ancestors?
- What events caused them sorrow?
- How did they react to hardship?
- What was the outcome of their reactions?

Ralph was *born* to Christian and Amelia Flygare 12 Mar 1905 in Ogden, Utah. The family was in mourning when Ralph arrived, because his eldest sister Alvine Margaret, age 15, had *died* just 4 days before. Her funeral procession was passing in front of the family home while Ralph was being born. Ironically when he died in 1955, he was buried on what would have been her 64th birthday.

Tip:
To keep the fibers in place, cut a small slit at the edge of the paper. Slide fiber through and wrap as desired, then tape to the back of the paper. Metallic thread, adds an extra shine to the page.

Though this is a tragic story, it puts the time period in perspective and reminds family members of the hardships this family encountered. it also reminds the family historian that these two siblings never met.

Elizabeth "Libbie" Campbell Hodge was born in Glasgow, Scotland on 14 Feb 1851. Her parents George Campbell Hodge and Elizabeth Geddess were first cousins. Their mothers Elizabeth and Annabell were sisters. Libbie and her soon-to-be husband John Shepherd Miller joined the Church of Jesus Christ of Latter-day Saints in 1847. They married 7 Jan 1849 in Kilmarnock, Scotland.

The couple, with their 3 children, emigrated with other Latter-day Saints to Toronto, Canada in 1854. Five more children were born in Canada. Libbie died 10 days before her 50th birthday.

The layouts on these facing pages are similar in looks, but the subject matter is drastically different. Be certain the journaling tells enough of the story for the viewer to know the difference.

Tip:
Metal objects, such as the spirals in both of these layouts, may not initially seem an obvious choice for scrapbooking. However, you will be surprised how many odds and ends you can come up with that are just right for some pages. Choose an adhesive that will hold heavier objects, such as glue dots.

Traditions

Activities, such as reading together, are perfect examples of traditions that are cherished within a family.

Children remember bonding activities because they bring comfort. Honoring positive traditions in a scrapbook helps continue the traditions for later generations.

Think about it:
- Is there something unique that your family always does?
- What everyday traditions have gone undocumented?
- Does a certain person have a particular role in the tradition?
- Where and when did the tradition begin?
- Are there traditional dishes?
- Is there a traditional game or activity?

Tip:
To get a more juvenile look, let a child design the page. Suggest to them a general concept. Be certain the photographs are already copied and cropped. Supply a variety of papers, stickers, markers, and embellishments.

When I was a baby, my brother would read a story to me on the night before a holiday. Whether it was Christmas Eve or the night before his birthday, he read something to me before bedtime. It only took my daughter once after hearing this story to decide to begin reading to her sister on the night before a holiday as well.

It was traditional in this family for the first grandchild to be presented to the grandmother within the first month of the baby's life.

Think about it:
- What simple acts were part of your family's lifestyle?
- Were there any traditions for showing off new babies?

Tip:
Current-day stickers can be used in heritage layouts by using one of the Distressing Techniques found on pages 22–25.

GRANDMA

RALPH

1927

FLYGARE • MILLER

ANCESTORS

In 1885, the widow Nancy owned a wagon, a horse, and 160 acres in the Peter's Prairie Community of Texas.
The following year, her bachelor son John rendered the property in his name along with 3 horses, 5 cattle, 12 hogs, 5 sheep, and $12 worth of misc. farm equipment. Mother and son worked the farm together until her death in 1892.

William W. & Nancy Yoakum Martin

Our todays and yesterdays are the blocks with which we build.
- Henry Wadsworth Longfellow

Legacy

HISTORY   Wheresoever you go, go with all your heart.

Tip:
There are a number of wood cutouts on the market. Look for thin, lightweight wood that can be easily glued to cardstock or tied onto the page. Unfinished wood looks great and authentic and takes no preparation time. You can also apply inks, or paints. Be careful, because wood contains lignin and the same elements that make paper acidic. Avoid placing wood directly on photographs. Use transparent protection between the wood and the photographs.

Even though it was not acceptable for a woman in the 1800s to have ownership of property, this woman took charge when her husband was heavily in debt and took control over her family's land and livestock.

Namesake

Laura

1963

1878

Historically, children were commonly named after a family member or someone in the community that was special to the family. The family hoped the child would follow in the footsteps of the person he was named after. Sharing the same name was to help him remember to follow good examples. When honoring your ancestors, nothing is more honorable than to name your child after an ancestor that means something to you.

Think about it:
- Who in your family has been named after someone?
- What was the relationship between these people?
- What traits and achievements were similar between these to people?
- Was there a family naming tradition, such as always naming the first male child after the grandfather?

Tip:
A wide variety of embroidery stitches can be used to add texture and interest to a page design. Another interest technique is ripping the paper, then stitching the pieces back together. If the paper is too thick to easily pierce a needle through, make holes in the paper with the tip of a craft knife, then follow the holes with the needle.

Constance Miller
1903
Laura Hennessey
1902

Constance stands next to a chair her grandfather made from the driver's seat of the wagon that brought her pioneer ancestors west in 1851. As an adult, she made the needlepoint seat cushion which is currently on the chair. This chair has been passed down from mother to daughter for five generations.

Tip:

Not everyone can own the same heirloom, but a photograph of the article will still preserve the story for generations to come. If it is not possible to get a photograph of it, show a photograph of the ancestor who is associated with the story and tell about the article. This will at least preserve the heritage.

Think about it:

- What heirlooms are still available in your family?
- What is the story behind these treasured objects?
- Who has possession of the articles?
- Are there any heirloom items that you or your parents were photographed with as a child?

Family Lessons

Ancestors have wisely given advice to their posterity. It is interesting to see a lesson come full circle.

Think about it:

- What advice or warnings were your grandparents noted for giving?
- Do you agree with their words?
- What morals did they stand for and support?
- What rewards have come about from listening?
- What consequences have transpired from not heeding a family warning?
- What vices and bad habits have generations struggled with?
- How have vices and bad habits been handled within each generation?

Tip:
When photocopying magazine and newspaper articles, include the title of the publication to give its reference.

This great-grandfather, who smoked a pipe all his life, gave up the habit and told his children to learn from his mistakes and never smoke. Three generations later a great-grandson burned to death in his house from smoking in bed.

This family was promised the blessing of always being cared for and never to know want. The story is told of them being forced off their land and being driven out for months. When they returned to their uncared for land, they were joyful to find a thriving wheat field ready for harvest. The family members have passed this experience on, and it has been an inspiration for other generations on faith and endurance.

Think about it:
- What blessings and promises do you hold dear?
- What uplifting experiences happened in your family?
- How would your family view this event?

Tip:
There are a myriad of diecuts and embellishments to choose from to illustrate a story when a photograph may not be available.

Our Wheat Field

My mother, Margaret Steffenson, left her native land of Denmark with her parents in 1853 and arrived in Brigham, Utah in 1856. Soon after arriving, she married my father James Hansen, who emigrated from England.

My parents took part in all the hardships and activities of the Utah pioneers. My father at one point gave a saw mill and 1500 sheep to the people of the community.

On one occasion President Lorenzo Snow asked my father for 200 bushels of wheat to tide over the workmen until harvest. At the dedication of the new meeting hall, President Snow told of the gift of wheat and promised my father "in the name of Israel God that he nor his family would ever want for bread." Soon after that my father moved our family south when Johnson's Army invaded the territory. On returning home to Box Elder, my father found a flourishing wheat field on our property.

Written by
Amelia Hanson Flygare
8 Apr. 1929

97

Clubs, Entertainment & Hobbies

Documenting everyday events gives grandchildren a glimpse into what a routine day was like for their ancestors. Facing numerous taxing and mundane chores and tasks, their ancestors looked for opportunities to find relief, personal satisfaction, and ways to stretch their minds and bodies from their normal routine. The interaction through clubs, various sources of entertainment, and hobbies gave such an outlet.

Clubs

People lived so far from one another that sometimes the only opportunity they had to socialize was when they met for clubs or parties.

Think about it:

- What types of social interaction was available to your ancestors?
- What clubs or associations were your ancestors members of?
- Is the club still active?
- Was there a group hobby or sport they enjoyed?
- Were they associated with a religious organization?
- How many generations have belonged to the same organization?

The girls belonging to this group were farm girls who chose to join a club as a chance to dress up and mingle with society. The words through the layout contain the actual club motto and theme. This information was found on the back of one of the photographs and confirmed by searching out the club.

ORIGINAL FORM

CAMP *F* *Weber* COM

Utah No. *3906* *Ogden*

THE SOCIETY OF DAUGHTERS OF
THE UTAH PIONEERS

Application for Membership

OF

Amelia Hansen Flygare

Wife of *Christian Flygale*

In Right of Descent from

James Hansen + 18 *54*

Margaret Hansen 185 *6*

The within named applicant admitted

April 8 19 *28*

[SEAL] *Cornelia S. Lund* Secreto

Both of these layouts show great-grandmothers with
their club members. Once you find out what "group"
your ancestors may have belonged to, see if you can
locate a depository of the club's historical records.
There you may be able to track applications, group
pictures, and what types of activities the group was
involved in.

Tip:

If your grandparents were members of a club, contact the club
about any past records. Obtain a
copy of their admission application
or photographs of them in the
group during a club event.

Eat your heart out

1945

BUTTON & Bogie

Tip:
Put your family photographs in time perspective. A wedding picture taken of your grandparents in the 1930s may not only provoke you to write about the marriage ceremony, but about their experiences during the Depression. A young boy looking "dapper" would want to look like the star of the era such as Humphrey Bogart. If your grandparents are no longer around to share such stories, there are numerous resources on the Internet and in the library to illuminate many time periods.

A club does not necessarily need to be a nationally recognized institution. Children have enjoyed starting and maintaining their own secret clubs with their best buddies. This type of information would need to come from family or close friend sources, as it most likely will not be in a published volume.

Entertainment

Entertainment has changed over the years. When a television set was brought into a home a couple of decades ago, it was a huge event. My siblings and I did everything in front of the television. We played, sat on our bikes, and ate homemade fudge straight out of the pan. We did not want to miss any shows.

Tip:
Whether the photographs are in color or not, bring color to a layout by using paper colors which are reminiscent of the room shown in the photograph.

Think about it:

• What did your parents and grandparents do for entertainment?

• What did your family do before "television" in the evenings?

• Where did your grandparents meet with their friends?

• How much impact has television had on your family over the years?

Tip:
Young people for generations have had "hang-out" spots to meet and interact with their friends. Honor the "joint" by designing the page in the same look.

Soda lids were used in the layout to represent the soda stand. An actual metal soda-bottle lid was smashed flat and used to mount the date as part of the layout.

Hobbies

It is hard to identify with ancestors one has never met. What were they like? What were their hobbies? their talents? their beliefs? This particular page lists the types of things a grandmother liked. This makes her more "approachable" to her great grandchildren, many of which have the same likes.

Tip:
Another suggested page would include a comparison between a girl and her great-grandmother.

MY FAVORITE THINGS

Nature:
- Springtime
- African Violets
- Horses
- Her pet dogs

TV Shows:
- The Edge of Night
- Masterpiece Theatre
- English Comedies
- National Geographic

Movies:
- The Quiet Man
- Shane
- Red Shoes
- Blues Skies

Foods:
- Chocolates
- Nuts
- Fruits
- Orange Tea

Books:
- The Classics
- The Story of Civilization by Will Durant
- Books on Classic Art

Music Programs:
- Saturday Morning Opera from the NYC Metropolitan
- Symphony classics

Sewing:
- Tatting
- Quilting
- Dress Making
- Knitting
- Bobbin Lace

Think about it:
What things were the same or different between a girl and her great-granddaughter:

- chores
- fashions: clothes, hair
- education
- talents
- interests
- friends

To further personalize this layout, authentic items from this grandmother were added, such as the handwritten note and the handmade lace.

My grandmother crocheted everything from tablecloths to bedspreads. This particular layout features the fringe from a blanket she made entirely from everyday string.

Think about it:

- What handiwork of your ancestors do you have possession of?

- How have you preserved it?

- How can you feature it in a scrapbook design?

Tip:
If you have an heirloom made of fabric, have it professionally cleaned before storing it. Wrap it in tissue paper to prevent it from rubbing against itself and from creating permanent folds and creases. Then pack it flat in an acid-free storage box. It should then be stored in the same climate controlled area as your cherished photographs.

Fishing

Gone Fishin'

Rainbow

Catch of the day

I do not know who all the people are in these photographs, nor do I know the date or place. I intentionally left blank areas on the page to add this information when it becomes available.

Tip:
Develop "a scrapbook page in a box" by designing a shadow box filled with memories and memorabilia of the ancestor you are honoring and what they loved to do. This box then can be displayed for you to enjoy and think of your family member and the activity you share.

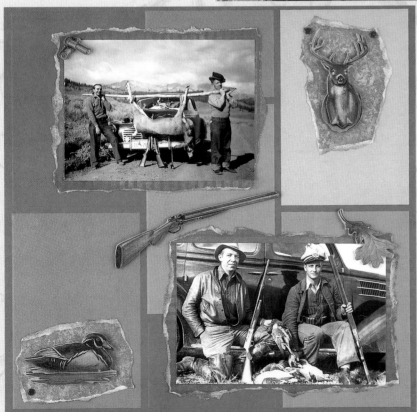

When you share an interest or remember someone for the things they enjoyed, you enjoy a special type of bond.

Think about it:

- Have you met the ancestor that shares your interest?
- Do you own any of his hobby gear?
- How does owning something from a grandparent make you feel?
- Why do you enjoy the same hobbies?
- Did you ever share the hobby together?

Sometimes friendships and hobbies are formed as children, and span an entire lifetime. Activities they did when they were young together may be carried into adulthood, especially sporting activities.

Think about it:

- What friendships did your grandparents have that lasted a lifetime?
- Why were they so bonded?
- Did you ever meet their friends?
- Could you tell why they got along so well?
- What affects did friends have on your ancestors?

Tip:

To create an active, interesting layout to match your ancestors' hobbies, create a design that is appropriate for the topic yet keeps your eye looking around the page. The fishing line wrapped through the photographs takes the reader's eye from one side of the page to the other while still blending with the page theme.

Ralph and Glen have been fishing together for over forty years. This hobby kept them in close contact their entire lives.

Ralph Woodruff Flygare

1912

Ogden Utah

Ralph & Glen—
fishing buddies
for life.

As you find historical family photographs, you may find activities that are not common today. For example, you do not commonly see grandmothers riding horses in dresses.

Think about it:
- What hobbies did your grandparents enjoy?
- Do your family members share the same passion?
- Do you have any photographs of generations doing a hobby activity together?
- What sports or outdoor activities did your grandparents do that is not done today?

Frank was holding a live owl by the claws just to show that he could catch it. He let it go, but only after someone snapped a photograph of him.

Tip:

It is especially choice to see family members in different generations involved in the same activity. While you research for information, inquire whether anyone has a photograph of an ancestor involved in a hobby or sport that you enjoy as well.

GRANDMA MILLER 1942

GRANDMA JILL 1995

GRANDMA FLYGARE 1972

GRANDMAS ON HORSES

Ralph called his

1923

automobile

"useless S. Grant"

Grant named his car "Useless S. Grant" because it was constantly breaking down. However, if you asked him today, it was still considered his favorite car.

Tip:

Memorabilia pockets can be used to hold items that may contain acid or other materials that may harm the rest of the page contents.

Think about it:

- What hobbies have your family members shared?
- Does the activity still exist?
- What is the hobby like today?

Household Duties

Your ancestors spent most of their waking hours in some type of work or occupation. Whether they kept house, farmed the land, or worked in a factory, they had a job to do.

The days of old were filled with routine chores. The basic lifestyle changed over the years. Some of the chores and occupations no longer exist. We don't have to churn butter or survey the land through a gun site. However, it is interesting to be reminded of how things were done "yesterday."

Tip:

Scrapbook kits that are available today can be fashioned to fit the era you are working with. If you do not have photographs, substitute drawings, stamped images, or a poem.

The poem on this layout was found among my ancestor's things, advising a newly married girl on how to do the laundry. I don't know if there is a relation to me or not; however, it does shed some light on how the living conditions were in the past.

Grandma's Receet

Given to a young bride by her Kentucky mountain grandmother.

1. Bild fire in the back yard to heet kittle of rain water.

2. Set tubs so smoke won't blow in eyes if wind is pert.

3. Shave one hole cake lie soap in bilin water.

4. Sort things, make three piles, 1 pile white, 1 pile cullards, 1 pile work britches and rags.

5. Stur flour in cold water to smooth then thin down with bilin water.

6. Rub dirty spots on board, scrub hard, then bile. Rub cullards but don't bile, just rench and starch.

7. Take white things out of the kittle with broomstick handle, rench, then blew and starch.

8. Spread tee towels on grass.

for Washing Clothes

9. Hang old rags on fence.

10. Pore rench water in flower bed.

11. Scrub porch with hot soapy water.

12. Turn tubs upside down.

13. Put on clean dress, smooth hair with side combs, brew cup of tee, set and rest and rock a spell and count blessins.

Cooking

The further back in time, the more families relied on home-made products. Recipes were shared with neighbors and handed down to children.

Some of my favorite recipes were the candy and confection recipes from my grandmother. She began in October making a selection of candies for the Christmas holiday. She would mail two full tins to us for Christmas. My father would hide one and we would share the other. Never has any candy compared to how good they tasted.

CANDY QUEEN

Think about it:

- Is there a favorite treat or dish that you associate with family? Why?
- Who traditionally made it?
- What were your grandparents' favorite foods? Why?
- Was it out of necessity that they developed a taste for something?

Signe's Pea Soup —
Yellow peas — soak over night —
cook + skim — add fresh or lightly
salted pork (mild ham) may be
spiced with ginger or sweet Marjoram
(no onions)

Signe's Sugar Cake
2 eggs — 1½ c. sugar (1 mix
flavor as desired — Melt butter — about
¼ cup — add to sugar + eggs — 1 coffee
cup more — or ¼ juice (milk)
if more butter used — 2 cups flour —
½ tesp baking powder mixed with
flour. Bake in buttered + crumbed
pan — 375° — Split + layer with fruit
build custard cream — whipped cream etc.

Tip:
Design a page preserving your favorite recipes and who they are collected from to ensure they can be used for many years to come. A recipe page could include a photograph of the cook, kitchen, or people eating the food; cooking tips; food quotes from literature; menus written in calligraphy; labels from jars and boxes; favorite ingredients such as vinegar, cocoa, pasta, and wine; or cooking utensils.

Tip:
When you are recording what your ancestors liked, be certain to add your likes and leave room for your descendants to add their favorites.

Leisure Chores

There are "jobs" that some deem chores while others would call them hobbies. Such activities have changed over the years from a job that had to be done such a planting and harvesting a garden to a hobby of growing a prized rose.

Think about it:

- How has gardening, sewing, and handiwork been enjoyed by your family?
- Have you learned their craft?
- Do you have any photographs of family members enjoying their passion over generations?

Tip:

When some photographs are colored and some are black-and-white, copy them all into sepia or black-and-white to keep the photographs balanced. To add color back into the photographs, hand-color various objects with watercolor pencils. Experiment with chalk, markers, colored pencils, or other colorants to find the desired effect.

For generations, the women in my family have enjoyed gardening and flowers. This layout shows five generations of women in their gardens or enjoying the flowers. I have my great grandmother's iris bulbs planted in my backyard. It is choice for me to see them come up every spring and think that she enjoyed them each spring over 100 years ago.

HONEYS

Chris Flygare
Keith Flygare
John Gillette
Jonathan Hall
Diane Flygare
Marianne Flygare
Richard Gillette
Robert Gillette
Julie Gillette
Robert Hennessey
Grant Flygare
Wendy Gillette

Ronald Flygare
Steve Hennessey
Nathaniel Hall
Chris Davidson
Andrew Hall
Mary Karen Hall
Laura Hennessey
Scott Gillette
Jeff Gillette
Danny Davidson
Reed Flygare
Linda Hennessey

Paul Flygare
Richard Flygare
Carolyn Gillette
Alys Flygare

Suzanne Flygare
Cameron Davidson
Carson Davidson
Alan Flygare

Ian Flygare
Lisanne Flygare
Robert Flygare
Mark Flygare
Brian Flygare
Nathan Davidson
Julianne Flygare
Michael Hennessey

Matthew Flygare
David Flygare

GRANDCHILDREN

My grandmother knitted, quilted, tatted, and crocheted. She made a queen-size quilt for each grandchild when they married and a baby quilt for each new great-grandbaby. This tribute to her seemed fitting to have all her grandchildren "sewn" together like a quilt.

Tip:
Hand-stitching on paper is easier when cardstock or heavy paper is placed behind the paper. This will protect the paper from puckering and tearing. It also makes it easier to keep the stitch even and rigid when sewing by hand.

Occupations

Depending on the era, your ancestors may have preformed some craft as part of their chores or for a living. Some occupations carried from generation to generation. Many jobs were dependent on where your ancestors lived.

Tip:

For an authentic look, use actual elements such as a dress pattern, misted with walnut ink.

These sisters were not dressmakers by trade but were just as skilled as some professional dressmakers and made all the clothing worn by their family.

Tip:

When possible use items from the actual clothing in the photograph. Be certain to deacidify items before placing in a layout.

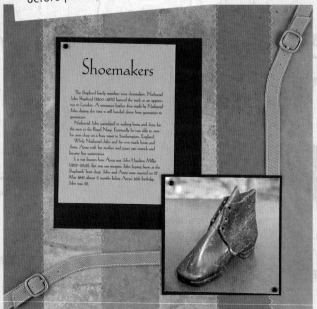

Think about it:

- What types of vocations and occupations were your ancestors involved in?
- Did it carry over to more than one generation?
- Are there pictures of their workplace available?
- Do these jobs still exist?
- Do you have a family business that has been around for awhile?
- Are you or anyone in your living family still involved in the same occupation?
- Did the job influence your family's religion, education, living conditions, living location.
- Were there historical events that effected their occupational choices?

This shoe was made by my great, great grandfather who was a cobbler by trade. As with a number of the trades, his father and sons were in the same line of work.

ABC'S and 1 2 3's

1922

Miss Miller's Class - Thayne Wyo

Ridges Studio
FRED C. RABE
416-24TH ST.
OGDEN, UTAH

58 59 60 61 62 63 64 65 66 67 68 MADE IN 69

My grandmother was a school teacher in Wyoming. All the children brought their horses to school on the day they had their class picture taken. These children were approximately fifth grade age.

Think about it:
- Did your ancestors get to attend school?
- What did they do with their education?
- Were any of your relatives teachers?
- What was a typical classroom like?
- What was a typical school day like?

Tip:
Using a white marker to represent chalk on a chalkboard will keep the numbers from smearing.

Homes

In the late nineteenth century, various situations caused families to move west—gold rush, famine, the orphan train, religious freedom, adventure, trouble with the law. Many families, when they arrived in the West, homesteaded their land. To legally gain ownership, they had to live on a certain piece of land and improve it for a designated number of years.

Think about it:
- Did your family move west?
- Where did the family move from?
- What was homesteading like?
- Does any family still live there?

Tip:
When little is known of a particular family or event, reserve a space for more information in the key once anything has been learned about them.

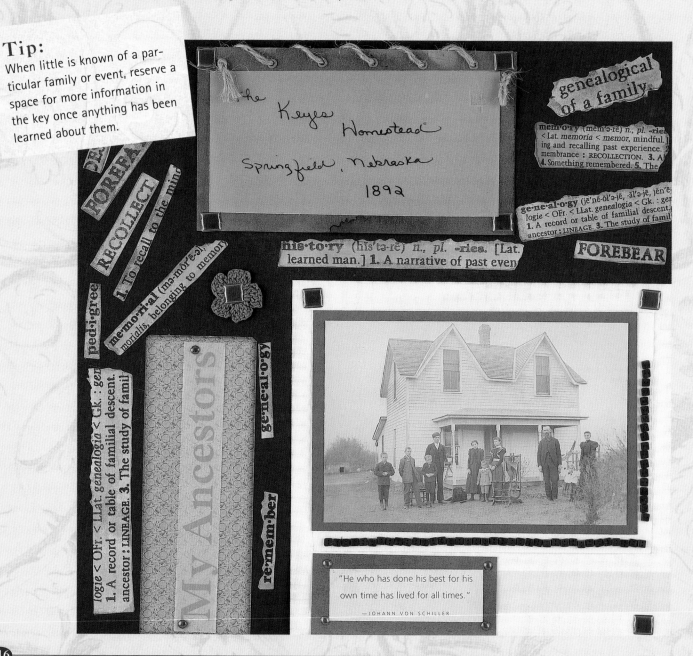

the Keyes Homestead
Springfield, Nebraska
1892

genealogical of a family

"He who has done his best for his own time has lived for all times."
—JOHANN VON SCHILLER

Once a homestead or an area was established, it was traditional to pass the land and house down through the generations. A farm or ranch could be run for decades by the same family. Many times the place of work was also a home.

Think about it:

- Where did your grandparents live?
- What was their home like?
- What types of houses have your ancestors lived in?
- Has your family passed a business or homes on to family members?
- Has your family passed land down through the generations?
- Have you visited a relative's homestead?

Tip:

Take an element out of the photographs and create a unique title using that topic. To fashion a swinging wooden sign, cut a strip off the bottom of the background paper, then reattach with twine, brads, or wire, depending on the subject matter.

It stands to reason that one's home would reflect what the did for a living if they worked at home. A rancher would have a great deal of land and a place large enough to house his ranch hands. A county commissioner most likely would live in town and have a conservative home.

Be cautious as to your ancestors' true occupations. Though Chris owned this chicken farm, that was not his job: he was actually a county commissioner. He ran this sideline to keep his children busy.

Tip:

To find your ancestors home, search the following resources:

- The U.S. Census Records list the location and neighbors of your ancestors' home. Check successive censuses to see if their home changed.
- City directories often listed the home address. Check the local library in the area where your ancestor resided for old editions.

Documenting your own living arrangements as a child is just as important to your grandchildren as your grandparents are to you. Think of the questions you have about your grandparents, then answer those same questions for your grandchildren.

Tip:
To hold fibers in place on the page, string the fibers through eyelets and secure with tape on the back of the paper.

Think about it:
- What was your house like?
- Where did you grow up?
- What influenced your family to live there?
- Have you revisited?
- Does your family still own it?
- What are your favorite memories?

Tip:
If your home is no longer standing, take a photograph of what is located on the land today. This will give you a perspective of the surroundings. You may choose to also add a drawing of what your home looked like on that land.

Character Traits

The accomplishments and things your relatives did for society usually dictate what type of people they were. Their actions may tell if they were hardworking, selfless, ingenious, and/or social.

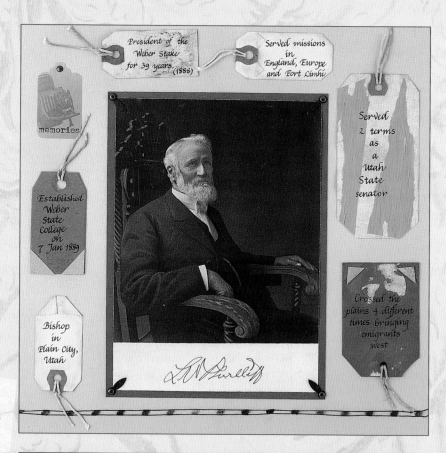

Tip:
Using the actual handwriting of the ancestors you are highlighting, brings a closer bond to the person. Photocopy or scan the writing to add to your layout.

Because this man had such a wide range of achievements, it seemed fitting to list his accomplishments on a variety of tags, all of which are one-of-a-kind in embellishments.

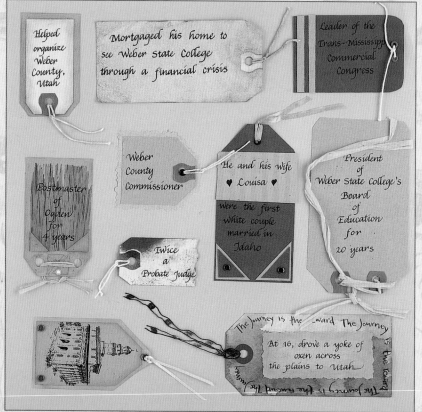

Traditionally someone with a lot of friends either knows how to be a friend or is wealthy and is surrounded by people who want something. Pay attention to who the associates were that your ancestors associated with. Why were they friends or partners?

Tip:

Buttons are a classic addition to a scrapbook page. They add a homespun touch to pages that are formal or casual. Buttons are easily sewn onto cardstock, attached with glue dots, or tied with twine or other fibers. How you attach the buttons may be more eye-catching than the button itself, so be careful of the focus.

This grandmother's friends were an important part of her life. As in these photographs of different groups of her friends, a number of them were actually extended family members.

Think about it:

- How did your family members contribute to society?
- How did your family contribute to the science, education, or business arena?
- What advancements are credited to your relatives?
- Do you have any photographs and/or documents of your relatives and their relationship to society?
- What ancestors have been the most influential to you because of their accomplishments?

Current Events

Pictures of the youngest members of your current family will become the heritage photographs of the future. Today's children are just as much a part of the lineage as the great-grandparents you are currently documenting. Giving these children a place in the album gives them a feeling of belonging to the family in the album.

If children have an interest in the album you are working on, they may have the interest to preserve it, share it, and continue the integrity of the album and the stories in it.

This layout was designed by my ten-year-old daughter Sara in honor of her uncle Michael. Traditions aren't just for grown-ups.

Children are creating their own as well. This little gal and her uncle have shared priceless times together. Whether he subbed as her partner at a daddy-daughter event while her dad was out of town or she acted as the flower girl at his wedding, the images and the bond they share will be cherished for years.

Sara purposely reserved a blank area on this layout to place a photograph of her and her uncle on her wedding day.

This layout was designed and made by my thirteen-year-old daughter Katie. The grandmother in the layout is her great-grandmother, whom she met only when she was a baby. The experience created a bond for Katie with this grandmother and she learned to appreciate the adventurous nature of this grandmother through pictures.

Tip:
When children are designing their own pages, they may need a little direction. Show them pages that you have already created. Let them know it would look best if they matched the colors and style if possible. Be certain they have plenty of embellishments and products to be creative.

Tip:
A paper-fashioned suitcase can be added to a page to hold a travel journal or additional photographs from the trip or event.

Think about it:
- What family members have a special bond in your current family?
- What ancestor had a similar outlook and personality as a now-living family member? How do they compare?
- What photographs are available of ancestors doing activities similar to people in today's generation?

Scrapbooking Living Family Members

Historical scrapbooking is not limited to people who are deceased. Living family members are just as important to the project. Interviewing and collecting materials from older, living relatives can add to the accuracy of the album. Glean from them information that only they know. For example, you will not read in a book what an ancestor's "lucky charm" is and why. This personal type of information makes family members more real.

Lucky symbols have been around for generations. The further back in history you study, the more you will come across superstitions and believed symbols for phenomenon the people at the time could not explain. This shadow box was based on a grandmother's lucky symbol of the penny. Every time she felt that she was in the right place at the right time, she would see a penny on the ground in front of her.

Tip:
When a symbol of an ancestor has a deep meaning or represents something uplifting, turn a scrapbook page idea into a shadow box; or frame the page and display it in your home.

I can't wait to be a

DADDY

Through the generations, many have shared the same dream: to raise a family. Little children, for generations, have pretended to be the mommy or the daddy.

Think about it:
- What did your parents/grandparents want to be when they grew up?
- Did they reach their goal?
- Did your parents want to be like their parents?
- What similarities have you noticed between you and your children, you and your parents, or your parents and your grandparents?
- What advice would you give to future moms and dads?
- What do you wish you would have known before having children of your own?

I can't wait to be a

MOMMY

Tip:

When you are connecting a concept between two different pages be certain they are similar in look and style. Be certain the color schemes work together, yet are different enough to show they are their own interpretation.

These pages showed the children in preparation for their dream of becoming a parent. The accompanying photograph celebrates their dream come true.

After working through the research done for your album, you will have a much clearer understanding of the types of questions your progenitors may have about you. Document yourself and your immediate family for their benefit.

Think about it:

- What advice or warnings were your grandparents noted for giving?
- What encouragement was given in your family?
- Do you agree with their words?
- What morals did they stand for and support?
- What rewards have come about from listening?
- What consequences have transpired from not heeding a family warning?
- Have you learned a new skill or talent because of the influence of a family member or a story about an ancestor?
- What do you wish you could ask a past relative?

Tip:
Make a tribute to someone who has inspired you. Whether you have met them, or their actions or words have touched you, keep this tribute available to inspire you continually.

My grandmother gave me words of encouragement to write, which I have taken to heart.